T0333030

Choose You

Choose You

Gentle Words to Help You Heal and Grow

Helen Marie

Rider, an imprint of Ebury Publishing
20 Vauxhall Bridge Road
London SW1V 2SA

Rider is part of the Penguin Random House group of companies
whose addresses can be found at global.penguinrandomhouse.com

First published by Rider in 2024

www.penguin.co.uk

A CIP catalogue record for this book is
available from the British Library

ISBN 9781846047787

Printed and bound in Great Britain by Clays Ltd, Elcograf S.p.A.

The authorised representative in the EEA is Penguin Random House
Ireland, Morrison Chambers, 32 Nassau Street, Dublin D02 YH68.

Penguin Random House is committed to a sustainable future
for our business, our readers and our planet. This book is made
from Forest Stewardship Council® certified paper.

To Philip, Georgia, Ella and Sammy –
my gratitude each and every day.

Contents

A gentle note for you: This book is a gentle, compassionate enquiry within to help you look at and understand yourself on a deeper level. Some of the themes may or may not be new to you, but when reading, if you feel affected by the content, I encourage you to put the book down and reach out to someone you trust. And if you find that some of the tools I mention don't feel comfortable for you to do, then please don't use them. My aim with this book is to be a friend to you and to support your self-work journey, but there may be areas that bring up deeper feelings within and you may consider that you would like to reach out for more professional help. I have included a list of resources to help with this at the end of the book.

Introduction

I don't know how long I've been searching to understand myself. Probably forever. I have memories of myself as a young child sat listening to my aunts and my nanna as they laughed and chatted about life. I chose to sit curled up on a chair in my nanna's kitchen not making a noise so that I wasn't told to run off and play with my cousins. The stories of their childhoods fascinated me. Stories of growing up and their relationships, as well as their belief in something bigger than us out there. Of course, I didn't know what that something bigger was at the time but, looking back, I feel they were all deeply spiritual souls with their own yearning for self-understanding and discovery. I feel that in me, too.

This wanting to know more found its way into my adolescence as I longed for more self-understanding, poring over daily horoscopes and agony aunt columns as if the answers would lie somewhere there instead. My teenage years, as is the case with so many, were a time of difficulty and identity exploring. So much so that I dreamed of being an adolescent psychiatrist, wanting to help others explore themselves with a desire to guide them towards feeling less alone in those years. I didn't go down the psychiatry route but it's no surprise to me that many years later, following marriage and three children, I went back to university and retrained as a therapist. I know now that this was something I always needed to do but at the right time. And it gave me so many of the answers I'd long been searching for. I will be eternally grateful to psychotherapy for that.

It's these answers – and hopefully some insights from both my personal life and my experience as a therapist – that I want to share with you in this book. It is my hope that it will help you facilitate a better understanding of yourself and of others. To help you find a way to connect back to yourself, to find value in you. To know that you matter, too. For many of us, we have grown up in a society that has not encouraged exploration of emotions, deeming some as 'bad' and resulting in us having to find different ways to cope without support in fear of being seen as weak. It can lead to self-sabotaging, self-abandonment, shame and poor mental health, where we neglect to choose ourselves or don't have the skills to know how to.

Throughout this book, I will take you with me as we delve gently and compassionately into the understanding of self and the various factors that have shaped us into who we are today. There will be a focus on crucial elements, such as self-love, self-compassion and self-understanding. Each chapter is designed to offer you a dose of self-clarity. Throughout, you'll find exercises and journal prompts to facilitate self-reflection and guidance on how to get to know yourself better. This book is about reconnecting with yourself, choosing yourself, so as to enable you to move forward in your life in a way that feels more authentic and aligned – a journey towards a safer and more conscious path – one where you ultimately choose yourself.

We can't always choose what happens to us in life, but we can choose how we respond, learn and grow. My own life, as well as the journeys I witness in my work as a therapist, have shown me this and I hope that within the words of this book, you will see how growth can also happen for you. And I hope that you come to a place where you can feel you can choose you, too. Because that growth, I hope you come to learn, is always our choice.

How to use this book

This book aims to support a gentle, compassionate enquiry within, with words to help guide you in your self-work. Being human is layered with complexities that can be difficult to deconstruct within the pages of a book, so holding an awareness of your own nuances, experiences and the context of your life may be helpful when reading. Within the following chapters, I offer you an invitation to gain a deeper understanding of themes such as emotions, attachment, self-love, authenticity, comparison, healing and, ultimately, choosing you. In each chapter, I introduce you to a narrative that will hopefully feel supportive and enable you to feel empowered in your self-work. For those of you who follow me on Instagram, you will see that each chapter begins with one of my list posts to offer context to the subject with examples that will hopefully feel accessible. I then offer gentle guidance on the topic, with relatable everyday scenarios and tips on how to become more self-aware and self-informed, and apply the guidance in your own life. Each chapter is packed with exercises, theory, definitions, journal prompts and quotes, all with the aim to encourage gentle growth where needed and a deeper connection to yourself.

Chapter One focuses on emotions and guides you through understanding your emotions and what they may be trying to communicate with you, how they show up in your body and tips on how to cope with the emotions that you may be finding challenging. It ultimately aims to put you back in control of your emotions and befriend them. In Chapter Two, I guide you through understanding your attachment style and why it matters to help you find a secure attachment to self and in your relationships with others. There's also a quiz for you to find out your own attachment style.

Chapter Three focuses on self-love with the aim of helping you explore why the relationship with ourselves underpins all others and why it matters. You'll be offered tools on how to practise self-love and be encouraged to start embracing self-love as the ultimate act of care to self. In Chapter Four, we take the themes we've learned in Chapter Three and use them to help guide you to find your authentic self and why authenticity matters. Think coming home to self and showing the world who you were always meant to be. Here we talk about the masks we may wear and the deep layers within as well as an encouraging section on owning your story as a transformative step in authenticity. We also explore intuition in relation to authenticity and how to listen deep within to the core of you.

Chapter Five is about feeling inner calm. It gently explores the ways our nervous system reacts to everyday situations. I guide you through understanding what a healthy nervous system looks like and there's an opportunity to build your very own self-care toolkit from the many calming tools that I offer within the chapter. Chapter Six is on understanding others and brings in the subjects of compassion and releasing judgement, and draws on some of the themes from earlier chapters to highlight that everyone has a story and, as a favourite forensic psychotherapist lecturer of mine once said, 'It's hard not to have empathy for someone when you've heard their story.' This chapter felt very important for me to be included. A lot of social media focuses on self-growth. Compassion over judgement for others matters, too, in growth.

In Chapter Seven, I guide you through what it is to heal, with an overarching message that we all deserve to heal. I include tips on ways that you can embark on your own healing journey and highlight the beautiful ripple effects of what it means to heal for you and those around you, as well as your future generations. Our healing matters. Your healing matters. Chapter Eight then focuses on boundaries, and I invite you to become more aware of what drains and energises you in your day. I then offer you ways to start implementing boundaries and tackle some of the difficulties that so many have in setting boundaries. This chapter helps you find a way to set boundaries with kindness. You can be a kind person and say no. Let me show you how!

In Chapter Nine, again pulling on the themes of the previous chapters, I explore why letting go can be so hard but fundamentally, for our self-worth, why it matters that we do. I offer you a ten-step plan to help you work through this as well as a personal favourite meditation that helps me when I need to work on letting go of something that is causing me hurt and pain. Moving on to Chapter Ten, I offer soothing and nurturing words for those days that feel hard. This is a deep self-care chapter that I hope you can come back to when needed. Self-care matters and I hope, here, you'll gain more clarity on its importance.

Chapter Eleven is on the hot topic of comparison. I help you understand that comparison is a normal part of being human, but I also dive into the detrimental impact that comparison can have on our mental health and wellbeing. Tips on how to come back to connection with self and what truly matters are shared, which will help guide you away from comparison taking its hold. And then we move to the final chapter, the heart of this book I have so enjoyed writing. In this chapter, I aim to illustrate the significance of choosing yourself. And, why, despite what societal messages you may have yourself believing, it isn't selfish. By having an understanding of yourself, as woven throughout the previous chapters, I show you how you can come to a place of awareness that you matter, too, and are worthy of choosing yourself. I will guide you through the process of choosing yourself and highlight how, from this place, you can enhance your capacity to love others. Choosing you matters more than you may consciously realise.

Fundamentally, I wrote this book as a guide to help you notice. Notice how you feel, notice how you react to the world around you and notice all the little ways that shape who you are in your day. It really is a book about noticing. And this noticing is a key part in self-work and choosing yourself. It's the starting point to guide you forward through self-responsibility to living a life that feels good to you, notwithstanding what life may have thrown at you. It is here to help you flourish to be the best version of you and help you move forward.

When I talk about self-work, I consider it to be an ongoing process of self-exploration to understand ourselves at a deeper level where we can really get to know ourselves. Know why we behave the way we do, see our strengths and celebrate them, and identify our weaknesses and embrace them with compassion. It involves a deeper level of introspection where we can learn to overcome our challenges, emotional wounds, limiting beliefs and any negative patterns of behaviour. Delving into the 'why' beneath so much of what shapes us can help us to come back to a place of deeper connection, understanding and contentment within.

Self-work not only helps us heal for ourselves but for those close to us, too, as we learn ways to have healthier relationships, develop more compassion and empathy, as well as hold an emotional maturity for those around us. Understanding ourselves can open doors to the beautiful gift of understanding others. If we see something in ourselves, then maybe we can see that it may be true for others, too. Humans are complex but through self-work, we can demystify some of the issues that we maybe haven't explored before and open up vast new spaces for learning. There's something beautiful in this learning, where, if embraced collectively, it could lead to new depths of human connection as we move towards encouraging the growth of empathy and compassion. Self-work truly benefits us all.

So, whilst this book aims to help you notice, it also encourages you to get to know yourself a little deeper with a central theme of compassion over judgement. If at any time you feel unsure or uncomfortable, I would suggest putting the book down, taking a few deep, nourishing breaths and only come back to the book when you feel able to do so. I know there is a lot to think about within self-work and meeting resistance in self-work may be your body's way of keeping you safe, so only go at a pace that feels safe for you. Holding an awareness of this as you work through the book is key. Get curious, but go gently. Maybe you could even reach out to someone who you trust, to talk things through if it's uncovered something you weren't expecting. Perhaps some of what you uncover about yourself here may benefit from some more professional help. I've included guidance at the end of this book to help with this.

As always, please know that you have the choice in how you would like to move forward. I have also included resources to help signpost you to articles around the themes I have explored, as well as links to my favourite podcasts, books and meditations. So, I warmly invite you to please delve in, start noticing, go gently, go with love, hold space for you to explore a little more and, please, choose you.

Chapter One

On Emotions

Our emotions may be telling us that
we can:

- have unmet needs.

- need to reach out.

- feel a little lost.

- crave connection.

- don't feel safe.

- feel misunderstood.

- need to be loved.

- need to offer ourselves compassion.

- need to come home to self.

Understanding your emotions and what they may be trying to tell you

Self-regulation refers to the ability to gently soothe ourselves when feeling strong emotions whilst simultaneously acknowledging and processing emotions but having the skills to cope healthily.

definition

Emotions are psychological states that we experience in the mind and body. They influence how we feel about ourselves and the way we behave. Emotions also play a huge role in our mental wellbeing, contributing to our mood throughout the day and informing how we interact with both ourselves and those around us. Whilst emotions can be complex to understand, it can be helpful to hold an awareness that they are neither good nor bad. When we learn to understand what emotions are at their core, in terms of what they may be trying to communicate with us, we can start to welcome them as messengers to guide us as opposed to suppressing, judging or berating them.

In this chapter, I will guide you through what emotions are, helping you to understand the wide range of emotions that exist and how they may show up in the body, as well as introducing you to the tools you need to process emotions in a healthy way.

Processing emotions refers to the understanding and gentle exploration of our feelings. It involves recognising and making sense of any emotions that may arise and allowing them to be heard and understood without judgement and expressing them in healthy ways. We can then use this understanding to navigate our experiences to help inform our choices going forward.

definition

Imagine a scenario where you are frustrated with someone close to you due to a recurring issue. Instead of lashing out and reacting to the issue or suppressing your feelings, you choose to listen to your frustration. Maybe it's telling you that reliability matters to you or trust and accountability. The frustration is rarely about the act but about the need beneath the surface. By naming that need, or by recognising the deeper underlying cause of your frustration, you can communicate with the other person. They may hear you differently when you speak from this perspective, as opposed to when you may have lashed out in frustration.

Suppressed emotions refers to the feelings that we try to ignore or hide instead of acknowledging them and expressing them openly. Pushing them down can lead to increased stress and potential long-term effects on our mental health and wellbeing, such as anxiety, depression and chronic health issues. Suppressing emotions can also affect our relationships around us as the body finds a way to express what we try to suppress. *definition*

This then opens space for further communication for both people. Listening to the frustration helps us move towards resolving an issue rather than getting stuck in unhealthy cycles that frustration may contribute to, such as ignoring your needs, which could lead to resentment and an issue not being resolved.

Fundamentally, emotions are an integral part of being human. Yet, there can be such a stigma around 'negative' emotions, such as sadness or anger, which means that so many of us may feel we can't express how we truly feel for fear of being judged, of being dismissed, to be seen as weak or that there is something wrong with us. How often when you were growing up did you hear 'don't be so sensitive', 'don't cry', 'you'll get over it' or 'don't let anyone know you're upset'? We may then grow up thinking that to feel angry or sad is a bad thing, and we begin to consider that we shouldn't feel or express it. So much so that due to many of us not being taught how to process such emotions as a child, we can become adults with all these big feelings and end up not knowing how to handle them, which can play a vital role in the state of our mental health. For example, we may be more prone to emotional outbursts, irritability, impulsive behaviours, self-destructive behaviours, judgements and harsh self-criticism. We may also find ourselves withdrawing from social interaction, avoiding difficult conversations and even engaging in substance misuse to cope with the emotions we are feeling but can't express or healthily handle.

Our core emotions and feelings are generally identified as sadness, anger, fear, love, happiness, disgust and surprise. Yet each of these has deeper layers of emotion, such as frustration, resentment, loneliness or grief, that can reveal so much more about our needs, our triggers and our desires if we allow ourselves the space to sit with the initial emotion and see what it is trying to tell us. Sitting with the emotion gives us the permission to witness the emotion as it arises instead of pushing it away immediately. It enables us to be with the feeling in a safe and compassionate space. It creates space for us to become more aware of ourselves, meet ourselves without judgement and listen.

- **Sadness:** may be linked to disappointment, depression, grief, loneliness, regrets, guilt or hurt and is often expressed through tears, withdrawal or low mood.

- **Anger:** often an intense reaction to feelings of rage, frustration, envy, annoyance, irritability and may manifest as aggressive or confrontational behaviour.

- **Fear:** an emotion to perceived threat that prepares the body for a fight/flight/freeze/fawn response and may show up as anxiety, people pleasing, insecurity, worry or helplessness.

- **Love:** an emotion that signifies care, compassion, passion, attraction and shows up as warmth, feelings of contentment, connection and boosts mental wellbeing.

- **Disgust:** an emotional response to feeling revulsion, contempt or offensiveness and can show up as recoiling, dismissiveness and withdrawal behaviours.

- **Happiness:** a positive emotion which encompasses feelings of joy, pride, optimism, satisfaction, elation and excitement and may manifest as contentment or calmness, and improves mental wellbeing.

- **Surprise:** can span both negative and positive emotions in terms of feeling moved, amazed and speechless, or feeling confused, perplexed, shocked or dismayed.

Although we may talk about emotions being negative (shame, guilt, anger, frustration) or positive (happiness, joy, pride, elation), both are simply communicating with us and all of them are normal human emotions. Positive emotions are sending messages that what we are doing feels good and provide us with information and feedback around what makes us happy or content. Storing these feelings to come back to and remembering what works to make us feel happy, calm or content can be useful for when we are feeling low. We may experience feelings of joy when we go for a walk in nature or spend time with friends, so we can come back to these activities when we want to move ourselves away from being stuck in less positive feelings (not in a toxic positivity way but in a deep responsibility for self-care way).

Negative emotions may be uncovering unmet needs, such as a need for connection, love and care, and telling us that we need to take more emotional care of ourselves by showing ourselves compassion or reaching out to someone. It's important to listen to both for the hidden messages they are communicating so that we can understand ourselves and gain a deeper awareness of what our needs may be.

> **Unmet needs**, such as our need for love, affection, support or a sense of belonging, can show up as emotions including frustration, distress, anger, sadness and hopelessness.
>
> *definition*

Sometimes our emotions can get a little mixed up and can feel very unhelpful at times. But if we come back to imagining them as messengers, we may find a way to connect a little more deeply to what they may be trying to tell us through taking time to quieten down the outside noise and listening a little more. Spending some time on our own to reflect on our emotions or even journalling are useful tools for this. Awareness around emotions and understanding our emotions as messages from our body can help us go from stuck and over consumed to understanding (What is the emotion?), processing (What is it trying to tell me? Where do I feel this emotion in my body?) and releasing the emotions (How can I care for myself in this moment and listen to what the emotion is trying to communicate?). When we understand that our emotions are not only telling us something but also offering us guidance in what we may need to do in the moment, we can move towards learning to honour our emotions and give them the space and action they may need.

Our sadness may be telling us that we feel lost and need to give ourselves the time to grieve and heal. Shame may be telling us that we feel there is something deeply wrong with us and we need to offer ourselves less judgement and more compassion and understanding (shame can heal in compassionate, safe spaces). Feeling guilt may be telling us that we regret our actions so it may be reminding us to repair a rupture. Anger may be hiding a deeper need to be loved, seen and understood, and reminding us to take a pause, acknowledge the anger and engage in some self-regulation/self-soothing in the moment. Feelings of loneliness may be telling us that we feel uncared for and may remind us to reach out to someone we trust. Anxiety may be telling us that we feel unsafe and need to use the tools we have access to, such as breathwork or positive affirmations, to make our body feel safer.

Self-compassion is treating ourselves with kindness, understanding and acceptance by acknowledging our suffering, imperfections or mistakes and responding to ourselves with non-judgement, empathy, humanity (recognising that everyone struggles) and self-care. It involves extending the same love and care to ourselves that we would to a friend.

definition

Listening inwards to see what the emotion is telling us can help with the action we may need to take. It's a deep act of self-care.

The body tells us about such big things in such little ways if we just take the time to listen.

I often ask my clients to name the emotion they are feeling when they are sharing something with me during a therapy session (i.e. feeling hurt, frustrated). And something magical often unfolds that is beautiful to witness. Most often, they are surprised by the question as if it was not something they had considered. We can sometimes become so storytelling focused that we find it hard to connect to the emotions and feelings underlying the story. And then, most often they stop, their words being silenced for a little while as I see them go inwards. And then the next stage always impacts me as I mostly notice their shoulders drop, their breathing deepens and they viscerally connect with the emotion they are feeling. There's often a quietness that ensues as they recognise what is happening. It's a beautiful connection to self as they then name the emotion with a gentleness that bursts with compassion for a wound within. There's less fighting the emotion or the situation and an acceptance that the emotion is telling them so much more than they first realised. This is the point that then enables them to see what the emotion may be uncovering and the need that they can try to meet for themselves in that moment.

This naming of our emotions has been shown to help the emotion pass as it enables us to identify what may be needed to help. Identifying our emotions and honouring the needs they are calling for is a beautiful gift to self as the process can help bring us back to a sense of ease and calm in the moment as we notice we become more in control of the emotion as opposed to feeling that the emotion is controlling us.

How your emotions may show up in the body

When we consider our emotions, it can be helpful to acknowledge the ways they may show up in the body. This can further help us process them, understand them and find tools to best cope with the emotion. Self-awareness of the sensations we feel, in conjunction with the thoughts around them, can help us develop the emotional balance to improve our mental wellbeing and contribute to improved mental health.

The impact of emotions on our body is vast and can lead to chronic stress, anxiety disorders, lowered immunity, poor sleep, gut problems, palpitations and change in appetite, all of which affect our overall emotional wellbeing and ability to be emotionally balanced and well. We may then find that these stored emotions affect our ability to interact with others as we become more irritable, snappy, withdrawn or even resentful. Not processing our emotions has a similar ripple effect to processing them.

Self-awareness is the ability to understand yourself by becoming more conscious of your thoughts, feelings and behaviours, as well as the impact they may have on others. Self-awareness helps with self-growth as you are able to understand your strengths and weaknesses, and see where you can make changes to better cope with both your own emotions and the way you interact with the world around you. *definition*

It may also be helpful to hold an understanding that through our body connecting with the emotion, it is in fact driving our nervous system's survival response of fight, flight, freeze or fawn (the tendency to avoid conflict). For example, if we feel wronged, our emotion of anger may drive us to fight to prove ourselves. If we feel scared, our emotions may drive us to run (flight). If we feel anxious, we may freeze to prevent ourselves being made more uncomfortable. And if we feel we want to avoid conflict, we may engage the fawn response of people pleasing. These are gentle examples of our fight, flight, freeze or fawn response in daily life that help us understand their core function. Emotions are an integral part of human survival. They are valid because their core purpose is to help.

Our autonomic nervous system, which is responsible for our fight/flight/freeze/fawn response, is also linked to our internal organ systems including our digestive system, our circulatory system, our immune system, our reproductive system and our hormonal system. And due to this link, we can start to see how our entire body becomes involved in our response to our emotions. Think accelerated heart rate in anger (circulatory system), think stomach ache in nervousness (digestive system), think skin breakouts in stress (hormonal system).

When feeling angry, we may have an increased heart rate, feel warm, experience red cheeks, muscle tension, spikes of energy, sweating, headaches, restlessness, fidgeting, clenched fists, rapid breathing, tightness in our chest, dizziness, clenched jaw, shaking or trembling.

Sadness can lead to lower energy, loss of appetite, a lump in our throat, heaviness in the chest, pain in the chest, difficulty sleeping, difficulty concentrating, a churning stomach, weak joints, slow movements and lowered immunity (more prone to being unwell).

When we are stressed, we may experience increased heart rate, increased blood pressure, muscle tension, palm sweating, gut problems (stomach cramps, upset stomach), fatigue, headaches, rapid or shallow breathing, sexual problems (disinterested in sex or erectile dysfunction) and hormonal imbalances, such as skin problems (acne, eczema or psoriasis), irregular periods, infertility, irritable bowel syndrome or metabolism issues.

When we are scared or experience anxiety, our body may show signs of increased heart rate, shortness of breath, sweating, trembling, dry mouth, difficulty sleeping, irritable bowel syndrome, and pins and needles.

And when we're happy, our body may respond by feeling lighter in ourselves (less tension in our body), we may smile or laugh reflexively, our muscles relax, we may find we can breathe more deeply, our immunity increases and feel-good hormones, such as dopamine, serotonin, endorphins and oxytocin are released, which contribute to feelings of contentment and overall wellbeing.

And whilst there is an abundance of information in our emotions, if we take the time to listen, this may be so hard for some people. Factors such as past traumas, fear of vulnerability, inability to sit with discomfort, fear and shame can all play such a role in finding it hard to listen, understand and process emotions. For some, professional help is needed to work with the body to facilitate deeper understanding and connection to self to hear the messages one's emotions may be trying to communicate.

I like to imagine the journey of processing emotions as nurturing the garden of my mind. Picking out the weeds so they don't take over the beauty of the other areas of my mind. Learning to sit with my emotions and listen feels like I am planting seeds of understanding, kindness, compassion and patience. And from this place, I can meet myself with more care.

Giving ourselves permission to feel our emotions (notice them and the sensations they bring to the body), sit with them and process them is key in helping them to be released and not be stored. Take a moment to reflect on how much better you feel internally when you've shared a worry with a friend rather than keeping the feelings locked in. The release is visceral and so necessary for self-care. The body feels it. This is a simplified example of releasing a stored emotion. Leaning into acceptance of our emotions can help us understand that we are not just an emotional mess but that we are innately human. Imagine, if we all accepted each other's normal range of human emotions and supported others through the ones deemed negative instead of judging or disregarding, the world would become a better place. Being on our own side here is a beautiful act of deeper self-care.

The science behind your emotions

Our core emotions are how we relate to and see the world around us, and they present as bodily reactions (increased heart rate, shallow breathing, tightened jaw). On the contrary, feelings are the conscious experience of the emotion (such as feeling threatened or feeling awkward). These emotional responses to our environment happen unconsciously and are linked to activity in the middle part of our brain called the limbic system. Here, there are several structures involved in the processing of emotions which, working together, process messages from our body via the vagus nerve. The vagus nerve is the largest network of neural pathways connecting the brain and the body, which runs from the lower part of the brain to all the systems in our body.

The mind and body also draw on the memory of previous experiences. For example, an increased heart rate might suggest to your body that you could be in a stressful situation because that's what happened in your body last time you were stressed. This highlights the connection between the mind and body, as the brain tries to interpret what the body is experiencing and decide what action is needed.

Interestingly, 80 per cent of the information along the vagus nerve pathways is from the body up to the mind and only 20 per cent from the mind to the body. Emotions, in fact, serve a deeper purpose: they prompt our bodies to react for survival, triggering our stress response, which includes the instinctive reactions of fight, flight, freeze or fawn (we discussed this earlier on page 27). These responses are largely unconscious and automatic, tied to our autonomic (automatic) nervous system when we perceive a threat or stressor.

Fight or flight response: a natural reaction to a perceived threat that prepares your body for action. Someone in fight response tends to fight back and stand up against the threat rather than running away, whereas in flight mode, the body gets ready to escape.

definition

Freeze response: a natural reaction to a perceived threat or stressor where instinctively you may feel you are unable to move or act and which can manifest as mentally shutting down and dissociating. This can happen alongside fight or flight or as an alternative.

definition

Fawn response: a newly defined defence mechanism whereby individuals try to appease the threatening behaviour of others to gain acceptance or avoid conflict. This takes the form of people-pleasing behaviours.

definition

The activation of a specific stress response depends on factors such as the perceived severity of the threat, past experiences, personality traits, cultural influences, context and current disposition. All of these play a part in which stress response may be activated.

How to healthily process your emotions

Emotional self-regulation is the ability to calm yourself down when upset and being able to give yourself love when you're feeling low. It is also being able to remind yourself that emotions are neither good nor bad but rather messengers. Coping with emotions requires us to have the ability to self-regulate. For some of us, this is a skill we learn in childhood from our primary caregivers, but for others this skill is not taught, and we may struggle to understand our emotions as adults. I talk more about this in Chapter Two on attachment and in Chapter Five, I show you some self-regulating tools that you could try.

Two of my favourite ways to approach processing emotions involve making the body feel safe and then moving to coping techniques. We can make the body feel safe again by using self-regulation. One way to do this can be by giving yourself the space to feel any emotion without judgement, whilst acknowledging that feeling the entire range of human emotions is a normal human experience. Then moving to coping techniques, such as deep breathing, journalling, listening to calming music, taking a warm bath or shower, butterfly tapping, movement or other relaxation techniques (more in Chapter Five), to bring the body from a stress response to a calmer state where you feel more at ease (if safe to do so).

WAYS TO SELF-REGULATE

- When angry, take some time out until you feel able to respond more effectively.

- When sad, find ways to express your feelings through journalling or being creative.

- When lonely, validate your feelings and offer yourself compassion as you would to a friend who was feeling lonely.

- When feeling anxious, find ways to make your body feel safer by practising some deep breaths, body scans and challenging anxious thoughts.

EXERCISE

Butterfly tapping

Place both hands out in front of you, palms facing you, cross the hands over each other and link your thumbs (creating your butterfly). Place your butterfly on your chest and start tapping your hands slowly right then left. This can be done for as long as needed until you start to feel calmer. Tapping has been found to help reduce stress and anxiety and promote relaxation for many.

Once the body feels safer, it can be useful to engage in self-reflection and ask yourself why you are feeling this way. You may uncover deeper thoughts, beliefs or needs that may have caused these emotions. Identifying the triggers here can be useful to help you gain insight into whether there are patterns to these emotions. If at any stage this feels unsafe or uncomfortable, step away from sitting with the emotion and revisit it when it feels safer to do so. You could also reach out to someone you trust to help you process and understand your emotions. Engaging your own beautiful power in these moments by reassuring yourself that the emotion is not controlling you and that you will get through this, is a wonderful example of compassionate self-talk.

The key is, when using self-regulations tools, such as breathwork, journalling or meditation, to begin to pay attention to your nervous system and notice how your body responds. Look for the tiny shifts that bring feelings of ease. Maybe your muscles relax a little, the tension in your brow or your jaw softens and you find you can breathe a little more deeply. Each of these accessible tools gives movement to the emotion, as well as bringing the nervous system back to a sense of safety. I always liken this safety to a deep, core self-connection. One where you accept yourself, are there for yourself and feel back in touch with yourself. As a wonderful teacher of mine once said, 'Look for the clearing in the wood and keep doing the things that work to create more of the clearing.'

Another tool that can be useful in this first stage of processing is creating some space between yourself and the actual emotion. So, instead of saying 'I am sad', which can make us embody the emotion in shaping our identity, it can be helpful to say, 'I am feeling sad.' This differentiation enables us to notice that part of us feels sad, but the whole of us is not. Notice how your body responds when you say this to yourself. Do you feel a shift? Maybe you notice that you take a deeper inhalation of breath, or your heart rate slows, your limbs relax and maybe you feel a little more connected to yourself, more accepting of yourself. Our body responds to the words we use, and our choice of words matter more than we realise. There's a reason why we say speak to yourself as you would to someone you love. You may start to feel calmer, and the emotion may feel less intense and overwhelming. A beautiful example of science and art colliding.

Once we establish a sense of safety within the body and feel less affected by the intense emotion, we can progress to the next coping stage of implementing change. This is not about ignoring the message of the raw emotion but rather ensuring that we are able to listen from a calmer state so that our response is one from clarity. Think about how you react to a situation when you feel angry versus when you've had some space to calm down.

Reaction (how we behave in the moment) versus response (our behaviour when we've had time to reflect, calm or regulate) can have a huge impact on how we process our emotions and, consequently, how we handle a situation. I talk more about this in Chapter Five.

Ways to implement change involve taking action and may include setting boundaries or asking for support. Maybe the action looks like taking time out from a work project that's causing stress, limiting time scrolling on social media if that leaves you feeling anxious or prioritising rest if feeling tired and overwhelmed. Or maybe you could choose to limit time with people who make you feel unsupported or have you doubting yourself. Boundaries are discussed in more detail in Chapter Eight.

Boundaries are personal guidelines or limits that people set to protect their physical, emotional, mental and relational wellbeing. They help people maintain a healthy sense of self and safeguard one's own needs and values. These boundaries can be around personal space, time and privacy.

definition

The RAIN technique to handle emotions

The RAIN technique was first developed by mindfulness practitioner Michele McDonald and is now widely recognised as an effective tool in helping process emotions. The practice enables us to work with self-compassion and helps us lean into self-acceptance.

Recognise the emotion you are feeling without judgement. This step alone can help ease the emotion. *Maybe it's anger and you notice the thoughts that are accompanying the anger. What feeling is it causing in your body? Maybe your heart is racing, your muscles are tense, and you may find that you can't think clearly.*

Accept that the emotion you are feeling is your reality so that you don't try to suppress it or change it. *Acknowledge the anger, invite it in and reassure it that you are holding space for it. Listen to what it may be trying to communicate with you. Try not to push it away.*

Investigate why the emotion may be there. What caused it? Have you felt it before? What do you need to do in this moment? *Get curious about the anger. Give it some context here. Where did it come from? Why now? What is it trying to tell you? Maybe you've felt misunderstood, or someone challenged your boundaries, or you don't feel heard or seen by someone and you're frustrated.*

Non-identify so that you do not become the emotion but that you are just experiencing the emotion. Let the emotion scroll by. A helpful visualisation that I like to add here is to imagine that your emotions are like the clouds and that you are the whole beautiful sky. Let the clouds pass by once you've listened to their message. *Remind yourself that the anger is just an experience in the moment to a real threat. It's valid, but it's also only a messenger to help* *guide the action you may need to take. Maybe you need to rethink a boundary that has been challenged or communicate your needs so that you feel better seen and heard. Listen to the message, the action you may need to take and then visualise the anger passing by.*

Journal prompts for handling overwhelming emotions

- What am I feeling right now?

- Where am I feeling this emotion in my body? What sensations am I feeling?

- When have I felt this emotion before? Reflect on past experiences. Is there a pattern?

- If I could name this emotion, what would it be?

- What are my thoughts about this emotion saying right now?

- What is the emotion trying to tell me? What lessons, insights or messages are there to the emotion?

- Is something deeper being triggered? How can I offer myself gentle compassion here?

- What action is the emotion trying to tell me to take?

- How can I look at this emotion from a different perspective? In what way can I reframe the thoughts underpinning the emotion?

- What tools can I use to bring my body back to a sense of safety?

- Who can I reach out to for support if needed?

- What steps can I take to soothe myself? What self-care practices are in my self-care toolkit to help?

When we offer ourselves compassion over judgement when overwhelming emotions feel like they are flooding us, our nervous system reacts in a soothingly soul-nourishing way. The shift is visceral. Our capacity to see ourselves as human can be a wonderfully healing gift to self in the moment. Can you find a way to create more of those moments?

Chapter Two

On Attachment

When we feel securely attached to self,
we can:

- feel safer.

- trust ourselves more.

- connect more deeply with others.

- feel more content within.

- experience healthier relationships.

- see our own worth.

- learn to not take things so personally.

- connect to our inner truth.

- lean into self-compassion.

- enjoy our own company.

- feel more empathic to others.

- see our own magic.

What is secure attachment to self?

Take a moment to visualise a scenario where you feel confident to take up space. And by that, I mean, space where you feel comfortable in yourself, to voice your opinions (with compassionate humanness, of course), at ease to communicate your needs and an overall contentment with being you. This way of being is the essence of what secure attachment to self feels like. In fact, secure attachment to self is an understanding of yourself that enables you to show up in the world with an inner strength that radiates confidently.

Secure attachment to self is based on attachment theory, which looks at the emotional bonds you form with others, described as secure, anxious, avoidant or disorganised. This theory also applies to the relationship with yourself. I talk more about this in the Understanding Attachment Styles section on page 51, and this chapter will help you gain a deeper insight into what secure attachment looks like in everyday scenarios. You'll discover how to identify your own attachment style, as well as some accessible tools to help you move towards feeling more secure in yourself.

EVERYDAY EXAMPLES OF SECURE ATTACHMENT

- Imagine feeling secure enough in your relationship that you can express your concerns without the fear of your partner taking it personally.

- Imagine not taking other people's criticism personally and instead viewing it as their perspective, which does not define your self-worth.

- Imagine not taking it personally when a friend cancels plans because you understand they have other commitments and it's not a reflection on you.

- Imagine taking a day off to relax and engage in self-care without feeling guilty or selfish, recognising the importance of nurturing your wellbeing.

- Imagine attending a social event where you don't know many people, and you engage in conversations with relaxed curiosity rather than feeling anxious about what they may be thinking about you.

- Imagine being comfortable with your partner having some time on their own or going out with friends, knowing that this doesn't threaten your relationship.

- Imagine not seeking validation from social media likes or comments, feeling content with who you are and not needing external approval.

- Imagine being at a family gathering where some family may have differing opinions, and you are able to have calm, interesting discussions rather than fearing them escalating into heated arguments.

- Imagine scrolling through social media and, instead of constantly comparing your life to others' lives, finding inspiration, whilst staying content and at ease with your own journey.

- Imagine having a partner who remembers your anniversary, but when they forget it one year, you don't consider it to be a sign of them not being interested, knowing they still care.

- Imagine waking up one day and having a bad hair day or having a day when you don't know what to wear and not letting it affect your self-esteem, knowing your beauty goes beyond your physical appearance.

- Imagine not taking it personally when a colleague at work offers constructive feedback on a project, seeing their intentions as helpful.

- Imagine starting a healthy exercise routine and sticking to it without feeling guilty about occasional indulgences or missed sessions, maintaining a balanced perspective.

- Imagine letting go of negative self-talk and instead embracing kindness to self and nurturing self-compassion.

- Imagine a friend being off or distant, and instead of immediately assuming it's about you, you check-in to see whether they are OK and offer support, knowing that their mood has nothing to do with your relationship with them.

This is secure attachment to self. Imagine. Even as I read these words, I feel a calmness wash over me, a need to feel more of this, to feel more secure in myself. And it's a work in progress as life shows us more lessons, more moments and more experiences. There comes a point where, if we are on a journey of growth and exploration, we may choose to delve a little deeper under the surface of why we react the way we do, and that never leaves us feeling particularly settled or content with ourselves.

Can you feel something shift in you, too, when you read these examples? Maybe you see some of yourself already in these scenarios. Or maybe you see areas that don't quite fit, and you'd perhaps like to find ways to move towards feeling more secure.

Maybe the following scenarios feel more familiar to you:

- Maybe you feel like you need your partner to constantly reassure you to feel loved and frequently seek words of love or physical affection to feel secure.

- Maybe you criticise yourself harshly when you look in the mirror and see only flaws, feeling only worthy if perfection is reached.

- Maybe you avoid discussing your feelings or needs in your relationships, romantic or with friends and family, for fear that you may be seen as weak and push them away.

- Maybe you find it hard to say no, concerned that voicing your needs makes you selfish.

- Maybe you constantly worry that your partner will leave you or cheat, fearing that they will prefer others to you.

How does your body react when you read these scenarios which indicate a less secure attachment? Do they seem more fitting for you? How do you feel considering the secure attachment examples compared to these? Personally, I find myself feeling more at ease when I consider secure attachment. There's a definite calmness within that has me wanting to meet myself with this love, care and understanding; wanting to value myself more. A feeling of quiet companionship to self.

A gentle note for you: If you are feeling that you may identify with a more insecure attachment style, please know that attachment styles are fluid and movement from insecure to secure is possible. The beauty of self-awareness, self-work and personal growth lies in the way you can witness yourself transform from a state of unease in your relationship with yourself and others to flourishing relationships.

You aren't broken. You aren't an emotional mess. You aren't damaged. You aren't unlovable. You may just need some gentleness to guide you back home to a relationship with yourself that feels more nourished, deeply supportive and understanding.

I show you this later, but let's first see if we can identify the attachment style you currently present with, whilst holding an awareness that attachment styles are fluid and heavily nuanced. You may also recognise aspects of yourself across different attachment styles, depending on certain relationships or situations.

I suggest taking a moment to reflect on each question in terms of different experiences and relationships. Maybe you can see how certain people or situations cause a more heightened response. If this is the case, take the score that reflects your most usual behaviour. Use this reflection to help guide you towarda a deeply honest answer.

Identifying your attachment style

1. When my partner/friend/family member is distant, I feel:
   a. Completely fine and independent.
   b. A bit anxious or worried.
   c. Relieved as it gives me more space.
   d. Highly sensitive and send my partner mixed signals of wanting closeness then pushing away. I often blame myself.

2. When I need help or support, I:
   a. Feel comfortable asking for help and trust that my needs will be met.
   b. Do ask for help eventually but worry that I'll be a burden.
   c. Rarely ask for help and prefer to manage things on my own.
   d. Sometimes seek help with urgency and sometimes struggle to accept help.

3. My self-image is:
   a. Positive and realistic, with a strong sense of self.
   b. Mixed and it depends on how people react to me.
   c. Generally negative but I won't allow myself to focus on it.
   d. Highly negative at times and I struggle with self-identity.

4. How do you handle rejection or criticism from others?

    a. See it as an opportunity for personal growth, if deemed constructive.

    b. Struggle with it and generally feel overly sensitive to any form of criticism.

    c. Tend to become defensive and withdraw.

    d. Feel highly sensitive and fluctuate between intense emotional reactions and withdrawal.

5. When I think about my past relationships, I often:

    a. Reflect on them with positivity and growth.

    b. Recall them with pain and unresolved emotions.

    c. Review them as closed chapters and invest little energy thinking about them.

    d. Have a complex mix of emotions and over-scrutinise and feel deeply insecure.

6. My ability to trust others is:

    a. Strong and I trust people easily.

    b. Slow to develop as I take time to build trust and often fear abandonment or hurt.

    c. Complicated. I find it hard to trust. I prefer self-reliance.

    d. Challenging as I fear vulnerability and betrayal.

7. When a relationship ends, I tend to:

    a. Grieve but can move on, knowing that I will be able to feel happiness in a relationship again.

    b. Struggle to let go and often try to keep contact in an attempt to rekindle the relationship.

    c. Maintain emotional distance and may act like I'm not greatly affected.

    d. Experience intense feelings of loss and fluctuate between wanting to rekindle connection and withdraw.

8. Do you believe that you are worthy of love and care?

    a. Absolutely. I have a healthy sense of self-worth.

    b. Sometimes but I need constant reassurance from others.

    c. I often doubt my self-worth with others, leaning more on self-reliance as opposed to relying on someone else.

    d. I battle this belief, having little self-worth and am sceptical of others' care for me.

9. When I make a mistake, I tend to:

    a. Accept it and learn from it with minimal self-criticism.

    b. Feel guilty and seek validation to feel better in myself.

    c. Downplay any significance of the mistake. Moving quickly on without reflection.

    d. Find it very difficult to cope with my mistakes. I'm very hard on myself.

10. If in a relationship, my partner spends time away from me, I:

    a. Feel relaxed and hope they enjoy themselves. I trust them completely.

    b. Feel uneasy and need reassurance but respect their need for space.

    c. Spend little time overthinking it and enjoy my own independence.

    d. Can feel heightened anxiety, becoming hypervigilant for any signs that they may want to leave me and seek constant reassurance.

11. My feelings about commitment in a relationship are:

    a. I value commitment and am comfortable with it.

    b. I value commitment but can sometimes struggle with it.

    c. I feel hesitant about it and prefer independence.

    d. I desire commitment but greatly struggle with anxiety around vulnerability and potential emotional hurt.

12. When I have an argument with a partner/friend/family member, I:

   a. Communicate openly and calmly to seek resolution.

   b. Worry that they may abandon me, so I avoid conflict.

   c. Withdraw emotionally or physically to protect myself.

   d. Have huge emotional reactions and struggle to manage conflict.

13. When I think about sharing my vulnerabilities and feelings, I:

   a. Find it easy and am generally open to opening up.

   b. Find that I can open up, but it takes me a while to feel comfortable.

   c. Struggle to share my innermost thoughts and feelings with others.

   d. Find this extremely challenging.

14. When someone close to me expresses anger or frustration towards me, I:

   a. Can handle it without getting overly upset.

   b. Can feel hurt or defensive but can discuss calmly.

   c. Do anything to avoid the conflict escalating.

   d. Become overly sensitive and struggle to manage my emotions.

15. When someone violates my personal boundaries or makes me feel uncomfortable, I tend to:

   a. Address the issue directly and express my feelings.

   b. Feel anxious about it but will eventually communicate my needs.

   c. Avoid confronting the situation and keep my feelings to myself.

   d. Feel confused and don't know how to resolve the issue.

16. When I'm scrolling on social media, I:

    a. Generally feel inspired and remain content with my own journey.

    b. Often feel inadequate.

    c. Frequently experience envy and self-doubt believing that I can't ever match up to others.

    d. Fluctuate between feelings of heightened self-doubt and needing validation to emotionally withdrawing.

RESULTS

Your attachment style may most likely be:

- Mostly As: Secure Attachment.

- Mostly Bs: Anxious Attachment.

- Mostly Cs: Avoidant Attachment.

- Mostly Ds: Disorganised Attachment.

These questions serve as a gentle guide for you to start to get curious about your attachment style and how that may show up in the various situations and relationships in your life. And there is, of course, a spectrum to each. Some situations may make you feel more anxiously attached than others, or avoidant, or secure. When secure, we generally feel calmer and sure of ourselves, more likely to be able to regulate our emotions, and we can optimally maintain our mental health and wellbeing through life's ups and downs. Whereas, when we are insecure (anxious, avoidant or disorganised), we can often feel dysregulated (uncalm) and exhausted.

Understanding attachment styles

Our attachment style is primarily shaped by our early relationships with caregivers. And each style significantly impacts our perception and experience of relationships, both with ourselves and with others. In fact, recognising our attachment patterns helps us cultivate greater self-awareness and makes meaning of the rationale behind our behaviours as adults. Maybe we can shed light on why we may value ourselves or why we may have trust issues with our partners or difficulties with communication and intimacy.

The theory, initially created by John Bowlby in the 1950s, focused on the significance of emotional bonds children form with their primary caregivers and their impact on development. It continues to be a widely accepted and fundamental concept in understanding human relationships and how we relate to ourselves.

Secure attachment refers to the healthy and trusting bond between a child and their caregiver. It creates a sense of safety for the child, knowing that their needs will be met, and they can rely on consistent comfort and support as they grow. This secure attachment lays the foundation for the child to learn to trust themselves, meet their own needs and, as they become adults, grow and form a secure attachment to themselves. The securely attached adult will generally be emotionally balanced, comfortable with intimacy and capable of having healthy, long-term relationships.

Anxious attachment stems from inconsistent caregiving during childhood, leading to uncertainty and apprehension about emotional connections. Adults with anxious attachment may find it more challenging to trust in their relationships and have a higher tendency to experience fear of abandonment and a constant need for reassurance. This attachment style can manifest as heightened emotional reactivity, difficulty regulating and understanding feelings and a need for external validation. This takes place because a secure base was not modelled in childhood.

Avoidant attachment occurs from a childhood where the caregiver was emotionally distant or overly focused on the child being self-reliant, which can cause the child to become emotionally self-sufficient and detached. As an adult, this can manifest as high levels of independence, often struggling to open up in relationships and express their emotional needs. They can become reluctant to rely on others for support.

Disorganised attachment is relatively less common compared with other attachment styles and is typically associated with a history of early trauma and severe neglect. These early experiences lead to the child not having a reliable anchor during development. So, as adults, these individuals often struggle with relationships as they are emotionally unpredictable and often exhibit erratic behaviour where they alternate between extreme neediness and emotional distance. This makes forming healthy relationships challenging.

A gentle note for you: Learning our attachment style can be fascinating but can also bring up a range of emotions. It can be helpful to remember that we're all unique and our attachment styles can be heavily nuanced and influenced by a variety of factors, including our early experiences as well as life circumstances. For some, gaining a deeper understanding of their attachment style can be enlightening and can guide them forward to seek help to grow and learn how to make healthier connections but, for others, this process can bring up past wounds or challenging experiences. So, I want to hold space for you here to acknowledge that this can be a difficult realisation. Be gentle with yourself as you explore attachment styles, reach out to those who you trust and please know that healing is possible. Attachment styles are not fixed. They can evolve with self-awareness and self-work. And please know that healthier connections for you can happen with the right help. It may also be helpful to hold an awareness that our caregivers were shaped by their own attachment styles.

How attachment styles may play out in our relationships as adults

SECURE ATTACHMENT

- Comfortably expresses emotions.
- Able to self-soothe.
- Depends on partner and allows them to depend on them.
- Honest/tolerant/close/trusts.
- Doesn't fear being on own.
- Doesn't require approval from partner.
- Positive view of self.

ANXIOUS ATTACHMENT

- Being alone causes anxiety.
- Negative self-image.
- Negative view of others.
- Requires constant approval.
- Highly values relationship but fears abandonment.
- Co-dependency.

AVOIDANT ATTACHMENT

- Doesn't depend on others and doesn't want others depending on them.
- Can avoid emotional intimacy.
- Suppresses feelings.
- Needs time on own.

DISORGANISED ATTACHMENT

- Displays unstable behaviours.
- Desires intimacy but struggles with trust.
- Struggles with regulating emotions.
- Avoids strong emotional attachment.
- Fears getting hurt.

There is a spectrum to all these, as well as cross overs with others, but each characteristic of attachment style serves as a basis to work from when considering how your attachment style may show up in your relationships. Even if you have a generally secure attachment to yourself, it's not unusual to experience moments of insecurity in certain aspects of your relationships. In these moments, it's helpful to be honest with yourself about whether your attachment style *is* impacting the relationship. As human beings with a need for connection, we may feel anxious if we consider our relationship to be at risk. Similarly, past experience in relationships or any experienced trauma may influence our ability to express how we feel in current or future relationships. Every experience you have is unique, including cultural and lived experiences, so what matters most is how you perceive and relate to your own experiences in the context of attachment theory and whether you consider something is relevant and worth deeper exploration.

Ways to move towards a more secure attachment

In therapy, the term 'reparenting' is often used, which means offering yourself the love and guidance that you might not have received as a child. It's a process that creates space for you to discover your self-worth, replacing feelings of worthlessness with a sense of value. It creates space for self-understanding, replacing confusion with clarity and kindness towards yourself.

The act of reparenting helps you embrace your uniqueness without judgement, as if you were seeing yourself through the eyes of a loving and kind parent.

Reparenting can look like learning to say 'no' when you need to prioritise your own wellbeing.

Reparenting can look like seeking out positive and nurturing relationships, embracing your flaws and imperfections, and understanding that you are worthy of love and care.

Reparenting can look like addressing your own needs and ensuring you're taking steps to meet them, whether it's getting rest, taking breaks, setting boundaries, moving your body or seeking professional help when necessary.

Reparenting can look like finding ways to understand yourself a little better so you can love and accept yourself a little better.

Reparenting can look like being patient with yourself and allowing space for growth and healing, just as a loving parent would with their child.

Self-work practices to support your reparenting journey

SELF-KINDNESS

Allow space for embracing your humanness in terms of accepting and celebrating the full spectrum of what it means to be human (cultivating an awareness here of your imperfections and your potential for growth). Practise gentleness rather than harshness where possible, whilst acknowledging you may find this hard.

Ways to do this may include:

1. **Positive self-talk:** Be mindful of your internal dialogue. Challenge yourself to replace self-criticism with self-compassion. For example, replacing 'I hate my body' with 'My body does so many wonderful things for me. I'm going to try to appreciate its beauty.' Consider treating yourself as you would a friend.

2. **Self-care routine:** Care for yourself as someone who matters, too. Establish a routine that includes meditation, breathwork, journalling and walks in nature.

3. **Set boundaries:** Practise saying no. Become more aware of you protecting your time and energy for what truly matters to you. Maybe this could look like spending more time with the people who make you feel most you versus those who drain you and make you doubt yourself.

4. **Forgive yourself:** Let go of past mistakes. And where you find this challenging, remind yourself that you're human and everyone makes mistakes. What have you learned from your mistakes and how can you move forward with this learning?

5. **Surround yourself with love:** Spend time with people who support and uplift you.

6. **Practise gratitude:** Reflect on the things you're grateful for and notice how your body responds to this practice.

7. **Self-compassion meditation:** Listen to guided meditations designed to cultivate self-compassion. Research shows that these are highly effective at helping you become kinder to yourself.

8. **Seek support:** Get proactive in building your supportive community so that you can share your feelings with those you feel comfortable and safe with.

9. **Be patient with yourself:** Be gentle with yourself, offering kindness when you notice any resistance and trusting that with practice, self-kindness will become easier. Look for the light.

SELF-AWARENESS

This involves becoming aware of how your childhood attachment may have impacted you as an adult, having created/formed some of your behaviours in your attachment in relationships. Be compassionate with yourself here. This is not an exercise in blaming caregivers (they had their own attachment styles from their own upbringing), but an exercise in understanding what may have been missing and the impact that may have had. It offers us a way to move forward and find ways to provide a healing path to more secure attachment with ourselves and those around us.

Ways to do this may include:

1. **Educate yourself:** Read more on attachment so that you can become more aware of what your own attachment style is as well as the styles of those around you. This opens up space for understanding others too.

2. **Reflect on your childhood:** Gently create space to reflect on your own early experiences. How did your caregivers respond to

you? How do you feel these early experiences have shaped your patterns of behaviour as an adult?

3. **Journalling:** Take time to make journalling a regular practice where you reflect on the relationships in your life and the part you play in them. I've included some prompts that help you delve a little deeper into this at the end of this chapter. Over time, patterns may emerge in your words that point to an attachment style.

4. **Observe your reactions:** Become aware of your own part in relationships. Pay attention to how you react. Do you worry about abandonment? Do you struggle with intimacy? Do you struggle to trust? This can help provide insight into your attachment style. Reflect here on the attachment-style quiz given earlier.

5. **Reflect on past relationship patterns:** Get deeply honest. Are there common themes? Are there issues that you feel would benefit from exploring? Were you anxious? Did you enable closeness? Did you communicate your feelings?

SELF-REGULATION

Learning to find ways to self-soothe (provide comfort) is an important part of reparenting as you may have not been shown how to do this optimally as a child.

Ways to do this may include:

1. **Become aware of your triggers:** Notice what activates an emotional response in you and notice what your emotional response is. Reflect on your emotional responses to different situations and relationships. Maybe you become overly anxious if someone doesn't text back straight away or maybe you fear someone is going to abandon you if they seem quiet.

2. **Challenge emotional responses:** Once you are aware of your attachment style, it can be helpful to meet yourself with compassion and understand that you may react the way you do because of the attachment. It can be helpful to replace any negative beliefs with more balanced thoughts, such as, 'Maybe they are busy, which is why they haven't texted back. It doesn't mean they will abandon me. That's just my attachment wound speaking.' Notice how your body reacts when you offer yourself this perspective.

3. **Develop self-compassion:** Meet yourself with compassion over judgement. For example, offer yourself the words, 'I am deserving of love and security.'

4. **Emotional regulation techniques:** Try some deep breathing exercises (inhale for a count of 7, hold for a count of 1 and then exhale for a count of 8) and grounding techniques (taking in your environment and using your senses to relay what you can see, hear, feel, smell and taste) to help bring some calm and regulation. These can help you to create a more secure connection to self in the moment. Take time to notice how these self-soothing practices make you feel. Notice the small shifts of feeling more at ease that may happen. This can help give you hope that you can make changes, that you can move forward. I show you more ways to bring self-regulation in Chapter Five that may help.

INNER CHILD WORK

Bringing to awareness our younger self and offering them today what they may have needed then can be emotional, insightful but beautiful healing work. What did they need to hear when they were younger? Can you find a way to offer them those words now? Go gently.

Ways to do this may include:

1. **Journalling:** Write a letter to your inner child. Address them with love and compassion and acknowledge their feelings and experiences. Offer comfort and reassurance where you can.

2. **Visualisation:** Picture yourself as a loving and nurturing adult figure and allow yourself to comfort your inner child. What words do they need to hear? What are they feeling? How can you reassure them? What comfort do they need?

3. **Reparenting exercises:** Consciously provide yourself with the care and nurturing you may not have received as a child. Maybe you'd like to gently hug yourself. Or cup your face in your hands. Run yourself a warm bath. Make your favourite drink. Watch your favourite movie. Look after you like you would with some-one you care for.

4. **Recall yourself as a child:** If it feels safe to do so, bring to mind an image of yourself as a child. Can you see yourself with empathy and understanding? Remember that your younger self did the best they could with the resources they had at the time.

5. **Therapeutic support:** For some, inner child work can be emotion-ally challenging, so please consider working with a therapist if you found this piece of work particularly difficult. Being able to love all the parts of you is important work in healing and finding secure attachment.

PRIORITISING YOUR MENTAL HEALTH

Finding ways to look after your mental health and the needs that contribute to better mental health, such as sleep, nourishing food, exercise, routines and healthy connections, is important in moving towards secure attachment. Holding an awareness of how you can best meet these components of your mental health is important. How can you create space to meet these needs? Who can you reach out to to help you with this? Where can you get support online also? Are there self-help podcasts you could listen to on these subjects? Are there blogs, articles and books you could read? Paying attention to what we nourish our minds with is key here, both in moving towards secure attachment to self and in looking after our mental health going forward.

And whilst some of this can be done through self-work, some individuals with more severe levels of insecure attachment will require the emotional support and guidance of a qualified therapist in attachment work before moving on to have the skills to offer this themselves.

A gentle note for you: Moving from being someone who may identify with an insecure attachment to a more secure attachment isn't a quick-fix process. It doesn't just happen. Our brains aren't wired that way. They developed from our childhood to see relationships one way and now they want to change. There may be years of creating a shift. It's a process of bringing the steps I've outlined earlier into your life. Letting them sit. Noticing what comes up for you. Paying attention to how your body responds and what thought processes come into play. It's about honesty with yourself and about self-responsibility, combined with a real want to react differently in the way you view yourself and the relationships around you. In fact, it's that want that can help bring the necessary action to move from feeling insecure to secure. And if there's resistance, notice what that resistance is trying to communicate. Get curious. Trust yourself.

Three gentle steps to help you move from insecure attachment to secure attachment

1. GETTING TO KNOW YOURSELF

Ways to do this include journalling (Tip: write as if no one will read your words. Get deep and honest with yourself), guided meditations and walks in nature to allow yourself the space and silence from the outside noise. Reflect on what you love and what you don't love so much, ask yourself questions around what/who inspires you, what did you always dream of doing as a child, how do you love to spend your days? Go deeper too: what do you wish you could change in your life? How about any changes with yourself in terms of self-growth? Maybe you want to change the way you show up in your relationships. Or how you show up for yourself and what you think about yourself. What are the things that you notice about the way you are that don't align or feel authentic? Who were your friends growing up? What role did you play in those friendships? And then thinking through a lens of attachment style, what characteristics of attachment styles do you display in the relationships you have or had? How have these behaviours helped or hindered you?

2. BUILDING A COMMUNITY OF SUPPORT

This is such an important step. The people we surround ourselves with matter more than we realise. Research shows that our longevity and mental wellbeing are dependent on the support network we have. The longest study, spanning over eight decades, by researchers at Harvard University found that positive relationships, both romantic and social, were the most important ingredients for happiness and longevity. More so than achievements, income, appearance, status or exercise. And the study found that those with strong social support experienced less mental health decline. The right people help lift us, inspire us, care for us, celebrate us, encourage us, support us and, generally, help us love ourselves a little more. Take a moment here to reflect on when you feel your best and who you're with at that time. Imagine the impact that has on your nervous system compared to spending time with people you feel less comfortable with. Talking through anything you're struggling with to people within this community of support who make you feel safe will also help you process your emotions instead of suppressing them. These relationships can help you experience feelings of secure attachment to self.

> **Self-esteem** is all about how we feel about ourselves and the value we place on our own worth and abilities. It's a blend of how we see ourselves, how accepting we are of who we are and how confident we feel. This self-esteem influences our thoughts, emotions, actions and how we relate to others. Striking a healthy level of self-esteem means having a positive and balanced view of ourselves without being overly critical or judgemental. Interestingly, our attachment style can have an impact on our self-esteem. Those with secure attachment tend to have higher self-esteem compared to those with an insecure attachment style. *definition*

3. BUILDING HEALTHY SELF-ESTEEM

There are several ways to try this, such as through doing something creative and getting into your flow. Flow state refers to that state when you're fully immersed in an activity, feeling inspired, joy, fulfilment and energised (and don't feel the need to check your phone!). Flow state can help build motivation as your body responds positively to the feeling of flow state. There's a beautiful moment that occurs when we are in flow and lose any feelings of self-consciousness. We can feel totally connected to ourselves in this moment, which is a wonderful tool for building a securer attachment to self as we are able to fully embody ourselves in the activity without judgement. Following the flow state, it can be helpful to allow yourself a moment of reflection and self-celebration of what you've achieved. This can be cooking a new meal from scratch, baking a cake or finding a new hobby. Doing something for yourself that you feel proud of is a great way to help you move towards building healthier self-esteem. Another key step in building healthier self-esteem is challenging your negative thoughts and replacing them with more positive ones (affirmations can be great for this as well as practising gratitude and noticing how your body shifts as a result). Other ways include helping others (community work and giving back can have wonderful benefits to boosting our esteem), connecting with those you feel safer with and caring for yourself. All these ways can move you further towards those feelings of securer attachment. Building self-esteem is one of the key steps in moving towards a more secure attachment to self as you create a stronger foundation of self-worth.

Affirmations to develop secure self-attachment

I choose to offer myself compassion over judgement.

I am not defined by my mistakes but by my growth from them.

I embrace my vulnerability and can see its strength.

I am worthy of healthy love with others and with myself.

I am learning to trust myself.

I am worthy of belonging.

I am worthy of feeling safe.

I am open to creating space for growth.

I release the need for external validation.

I choose to embrace self-compassion.

I may not know how, but I will find a way.

I am choosing to embrace my authentic self.

The right people will love me for who I am.

I trust that I can be the person I need.

I choose to acknowledge that I matter, too.

Journal prompts for developing a secure sense of self

- What is your self-talk like? How does it make your body feel? How would you like to talk to yourself? What ways can you try?

- What are some self-limiting beliefs you have about yourself? How can you challenge them? What positive affirmations can you replace them with?

- How do you show up in your relationships? Are there any changes you would like to make? And if so, what would these changes look like?

- What matters to you? What are your core values and beliefs?

- What are your needs? How are you currently meeting them? How could you meet them more?

- How can you be the person you need to care for you?

- What words of guidance and compassion can you give yourself to help you feel more secure in yourself and in your relationships?

- What things make you feel deeply connected to yourself? What sensations do you notice in your body? How can you create more space for this?

- What's one small step you can take today to work on your sense of self?

The relationship with yourself can be extremely complex but as you journey through this process of self-honesty and your awareness blooms in response to the deeper conversations you have with yourself, you can create space to find new ways to love yourself a little deeper. You can create new ways to trust yourself a little deeper. And new ways to find a deeper level of beautiful peace within.

On Self-Love

Chapter Three

You deserve to:

- feel that you matter, too.

- talk to yourself with kindness.

- forgive yourself for past mistakes.

- grow/evolve/bloom.

- trust yourself.

- like yourself.

- meet your own needs.

- accept yourself.

- be there for yourself.

- treat yourself like someone you love.

What is self-love?

> **Self-love** is the gentle embracing of our own worthiness and inherent value. It is the nurturing self-practice of compassion, forgiveness, acceptance and honouring of our needs.
>
> *definition*

Imagine being on your own side. Imagine being the person you need in your life. This is how I imagine self-love. It is a beautiful way of being there for yourself, offering compassion over judgement and leaning into a mindset that says, 'I matter, too.' It could be embracing our moments of vulnerability and offering soothing words. It could be nurturing rituals that replenish your soul, such as taking a bath, immersing yourself in nature or savouring a moment of stillness for yourself with a warm drink. It could be cultivating a practice of self-forgiveness and acknowledging that making mistakes is part of being human. It could be offering yourself the same words of kindness you would offer to a friend who was struggling in the moment.

At its core, self-love is a deep nourishing act of self-acceptance of our humanness.

Acknowledging our humanness encompasses our imperfections, vulnerabilities and complexities whilst holding a recognition that we are not meant to be flawless; we are meant to be human with all that humanness entails. Such as making mistakes, facing setbacks, experiencing the full spectrum of emotions from joy to love to sadness and anger, which are all a natural part of being human, needing to rest, needing to connect with others, needing to feel that we belong and needing to feel accepted. Self-love is about truly embracing what it is to be human.

Take a moment here to notice how you feel when you criticise yourself: 'I'm so stupid, I shouldn't have done that.' What sensations do you notice? Some tension maybe? Or some irritation? Now consider offering yourself compassion: 'It's OK to make mistakes, that's part of being human. What can I learn from this going forward?' What sensations did you notice here? By offering this compassion, you may notice your body soften in gratitude. From this place, we may begin to feel safer to be us. And it's from this place that we may be able to offer ourselves support, guidance and nurturing. Of course, self-love looks different for everyone, but it's a way of being there for yourself and taking care of your needs in a way that feels right for you. Consider it as a deep, honest conversation with yourself on how to look after yourself holistically to encompass both your physical and emotional needs.

Self-compassion is the tender practice of offering ourselves understanding, especially in moments where we are struggling or in pain. It involves embracing our imperfections and accepting them as part of being human. Self-compassion is the antidote to self-judgement.

definition

Let's take another moment. Can you connect with yourself and reflect on what your needs are right now? Allow yourself to pause and listen inwards. We so rarely take the time to ask ourselves this question although it's a precious act of self-love to listen inwards to gain clarity of what our needs may be and offer ourselves ways to meet them. Maybe you'll find a need for rest, or a longing for letting go of something. Or maybe it's a need for slowing down and creating space for you, or a need for more joy, laughter and connection. But listen. Take a moment to connect within. Maybe take five minutes to jot down some of those needs to come back to later. Fundamentally, even though it may at times be hard to identify your needs, you will generally know what they are over someone else who isn't you. You know yourself best, even if it may take some deeper work and tapping into self-awareness to get to know yourself a little more. Identifying your needs and learning how to meet them is a key step in self-love.

Our physical needs can look like:

- Keeping hydrated.

- Eating nourishing food.

- Having a safe place to live.

- Having appropriate clothes for warmth and comfort.

- Keeping fit and active.

- Maintaining our hygiene.

- Getting adequate sleep and rest.

- Having access to healthcare.

- Creating a safe environment around us.

- Feeling a safe connection with others.

Our emotional needs can look like:

- Having a strong support network.

- Experiencing love and affection.

- Feeling like we belong.

- Feeling respected.

- Feeling safe and secure.

- Having trustworthy relationships.

- Being able to give ourselves validation.

- Feeling seen and heard.

- Having autonomy and independence.

- Having a purpose.

- Feeling accepted.

- Having emotional connections.

- Being able to express ourselves.

- Being able to experience intimacy.

- Having space and privacy.

- Sharing compassion and empathy.

- Being able to grow and evolve.

Embracing the practice of self-love can be challenging, especially if we were not exposed to healthy examples of this whilst growing up. Perhaps we were not shown how to prioritise our needs, or how to identify them, or maybe we were even actively discouraged not to. The way we have learned to take care, or not take care, of ourselves is so often deeply rooted in our early childhood experiences. Additionally, there may have been societal messages and cultural influences that deemed self-love and care as being selfish. Maybe we received messages that we needed to be perfect, that rest is for the weak, or that showing our emotions was not what we should do, that we should always meet others' needs over our own.

However, understanding where your own beliefs about self-love come from can be a helpful first step in challenging them. Resisting self-love can often be explained by the self-limiting messages that we received growing up. Maybe you were told that self-love was selfish. Maybe you were encouraged to think that it was for the weak. Or maybe you weren't shown healthy examples of self-love growing up. But are these beliefs helping you flourish? Are they helping you feel aligned, at peace and fulfilled? This process of reflecting on these questions can help you redefine your relationship with self-love so that you can learn to offer yourself the love, care and compassion that will help you on a journey towards inner peace and ease. It can also help you move from seeing self-love as inherently selfish to seeing that it is a delicate balance between meeting our own needs as well as those of others. It's harmoniously both.

If you are unable to show yourself love, you may develop thought processes where you don't think you matter, make unhealthy choices, find yourself people pleasing, neglect yourself, don't consider your needs to be important, dismiss your feelings, don't respect yourself, speak unkindly to yourself, judge yourself and don't prioritise yourself when needed. This in turn can contribute to poor emotional health and may also result in poor physical health because when we struggle to meet our needs, we may develop symptoms of anxiety, depression and chronic stress. These may manifest as persistent worry, racing thoughts, difficulty sleeping, headaches, feeling overwhelmed, low energy, irritability or withdrawing from friends and family. All of which can have an impact on both our body and our mind. Self-love matters more than we consciously realise.

If you meet yourself with love, you give yourself a better chance of showing up as the best version of yourself. With this, you can develop healthier relationships, be more present, value yourself and, in turn, value others and show up more authentically, which boosts wellbeing.

Consider a day when you didn't feel good about yourself. Were you meeting yourself with compassion? How was your self-talk? Were you letting your negative thoughts spiral? How did this affect how you were able to show up for yourself and for others. I know, for me, that when I feel like this, I'm less able to be present and enjoy my time with others. I feel more on edge and less connected to myself. This isn't a version of me that feels loved and cared for and it can sometimes make me feel quite isolated and alone in my thoughts. How about you? How have those days made you feel?

When you come from a place of self-love, you will often feel better about yourself. This showing up from a place of self-love can have a positive impact on the environment you may find yourself in, creating a beautiful ripple effect. This may manifest in your relationships when you're more present and feel more connected to the people around you, filling your cup with the goodness that will help you cope better with the challenges in life.

Of course, this cannot happen all the time and self-love is not something you can easily turn on. It is something that you cultivate with awareness, practice, reflection and self-review of what works and what doesn't work. Embracing self-love requires you to meet yourself at a place of self-understanding with a commitment to self-growth. It involves challenging self-limiting beliefs, releasing self-blame, guilt, low self-worth, low self-esteem through gently extending kindness and compassion to yourself and holding an awareness that you do intrinsically matter, so that you can nurture healthier relationships with yourself and those around you. Remember it's a gentle process that takes time. I think this is something we shouldn't overlook.

Self-understanding is the beautiful journey of exploring a little deeper into who we are, and unravelling the layers beneath our thoughts, emotions and experiences that shape who we are. It involves meeting ourselves with gentle curiosity so as to gain clarity and deeper connection to the essence of what being us means. *definition*

Take a moment here to reflect on what self-love means to you and what small steps you could take to implement some kindness to yourself today. Maybe take five minutes out to stretch when you're at your desk, instead of pushing through, or call a friend if you're feeling a little low. Think tiny steps of self-love and keep building on them. Think being on your own side. Think being the person you need to care for you in the moment.

It's time to take a gentle, compassionate enquiry within. With a little dose of courage, and gentle curiosity, you can start to question your belief system around self-love. Maybe you will start to see glimmers of ways to move forward and hear the whispers deep within guiding you towards what you really need. Maybe you'll come to a place of self-love that will move you in ways that not showing self-love ever will. Maybe you'll notice how the gentle acts of caring for yourself are starting to have a positive effect, however small, and you'll become keen to keep adding to them. Then gently, over time, you may come to a place of wanting to show yourself love instead of fighting to love yourself, so that the practice of self-love will at least stand a chance of becoming ever so slightly easier to embrace.

How to practise self-love

1. CHECK-IN WITH YOURSELF

How are you feeling? Happy? Sad? Low? Demotivated? Resentful? Remember from Chapter One, we are meant to feel all the spectrum of emotions. None are to be labelled good or bad. So, what are your emotions saying? What's behind the feeling? Get curious. Get compassionate. Be gentle. Take a moment to connect with how your body feels and what it may be telling you. What are your thoughts saying? Are they negative or positive? Can you reframe them? What do you need in this moment? How can you look after yourself? Getting into the practice of connecting with yourself like this regularly can bring a deeper level of noticing, which can help you become more aware of your needs also.

2. THINK ABOUT WHERE YOUR ENERGY GOES EACH DAY

Energy is the essence of our inner resources and the focus of our attention and efforts. It is our precious life currency and we should be mindful of where we spend it. I talk more about this in Chapter Eight. So, take a moment to reflect on whether you are feeling inspired? Are you feeling drained? Noticing how you feel each day around the things that you do and the people you spend time with can be a helpful starting point for bringing awareness to the changes you may like to make to live a life that feels more inspiring. This could be noticing that you make little time for self-care and accordingly starting to create space for yourself in your week. Or maybe it could mean spending more time with those who nourish, inspire and lift you over those who make you feel drained. Or it could be identifying that you feel most at peace when involved in a creative project, so you make more time for that. Remember that nothing changes if nothing changes. So, if you continue to not reflect on where your energy goes, you may repeatedly feel exhausted and drained. Bring consciousness to the beautiful currency that is yours to choose how you spend it.

3. ADD MOVEMENT TO YOUR DAY

Movement helps release feel-good hormones, which can boost our mental wellbeing and make us feel less stressed and anxious, as well as help us cope with any negative thoughts we may be having. This can be a walk in nature, a gym class, yoga, a gentle stretch at your desk or a dance around to your favourite songs. Have you noticed how your perspective shifts on something when you've moved your body? The process of movement can be incredibly beneficial when we are feeling stuck in our thoughts and need some help to move them forward and away from negative rumination.

4. MEDITATE

Giving ourselves the space to create a moment of calm in our day can help long term with improved self-awareness and self-esteem. Meditation has been proven to help reduce symptoms of stress and anxiety, such as spiralling thoughts, worry and tension, as well as to enable us to make better choices for ourselves, be kinder to ourselves and improve our physical health as it helps to lower blood pressure, encourages better sleep, induces relaxation of any muscle tension and even helps with reducing chronic pain. It can take the form of guided meditations in stillness, walking meditations, sleep meditations or simple soundscapes to help you relax.

5. OFFER YOURSELF COMPASSION OVER JUDGEMENT

How is your self-talk? Do you meet yourself with care? Or are you harsh? How would it feel to speak kindly to yourself when you're struggling? I doubt that judging yourself has helped. In fact, it can be an isolating place to be when we meet ourselves with judgement. Self-compassion can help bring you back to being on your own side. Hold an awareness that this is a process and takes practice but that it can help you meet yourself from a place of self-love. This can include forgiving yourself for past mistakes by gently acknowledging that we are human and we all make mistakes. What have you learned about your past mistakes, your judgement, your harshness? Can you use these experiences to cultivate growth and gentleness? Can you use the lessons to move forward in a way that feels more beautiful for you? Reflection with gentleness and compassion can be so healing in the moment. We are all human. We are humans who feel, and who learn as we move through this path of life. How can you make it a path of compassion?

6. JOURNAL

Writing like no one will read your words can be an incredibly cathartic and soothing practice. This can be through following guided journal prompts, such as those included at the end of each chapter in this book, or simply writing how you feel and what is on your mind. This act of putting pen to paper helps give movement to our emotions and helps release them from being stored in the body where they can manifest as stress and anxiety. Journalling also benefits our mental health by enabling us to track our mood and identify concerns that we may need help with. I like to think of it as a decluttering of the mind.

7. SET PERSONAL BOUNDARIES

I talk more in depth about boundaries in Chapter Eight, but boundaries are the gentle yet firm lines we draw to protect our mental wellbeing. How could you use boundaries to protect you a little more? What limits could you set? What priorities can you make? These self-boundaries can help us make healthier choices in our life, such as what we say no to, how we choose to spend our time, not pressing play on one more episode of Netflix when it's late already and we have work in the morning, not drunk texting, not keeping tabs on people, creating personal space, not checking work emails at the weekend, and so on. All beautiful acts of self-love that we may not consciously realise.

8. NOURISH YOUR MIND, BODY AND SOUL

Think about the things that make you feel nourished, such as being deeply present in the activities that you're doing, that first sip of coffee, taking a moment for you, reading a good book, learning something new, limiting screentime, getting fresh air and sticking to a sleep routine. Can you look at ways to also add in meditation, journalling, walks in nature and movement? These are all ways to strengthen our relationship with ourselves, a key component of self-love.

9. LET GO OF COMPARISON

This is covered in more depth in Chapter Eleven, but here is a gentle reminder that comparison takes you away from focusing on yourself and can take you to a place of feeling less than other people. It takes you away from living your life. Working on finding a way to bring it back to you (such as focusing on what you've achieved) as well as holding an awareness that we never know someone's full story and we see only what they may choose to show us can be helpful here. Can you take a moment to focus on what matters to you, adding in things that make you feel good about being you, such as the life you've built for yourself, the struggles you've gone through and something you're proud of? This can help shift to feelings of fulfilment that comparison can never bring, unless we think of using comparison as inspiration and I talk about this more in Chapter Eleven. The practice of gratitude here can be a good practice when you find yourself caught in the comparison trap as it facilitates the release of feel-good hormones, which bring feelings of ease as opposed to the stress hormones that comparison can induce, which can leave us feeling frustrated, irritated, lethargic and fatigued.

10. CREATE SPACE FOR YOURSELF

Dedicating time for you is an important part of self-love. It enables us to put self-love into our daily routine. You could schedule time in your diary to keep free for something of your choice in the moment, be it reading a book, taking a walk, calling a friend or simply turning your phone off for an hour. Schedule time for joy. Using this space to just be with ourselves for a while, to quieten the mind and to connect back within can help us hear ourselves a little more. This act of creating space helps build resilience, which refers to our inner energy resources that help us cope better with the day-to-day demands of what life may bring. I talk more about this in Chapter Eight.

If self-love is something new for you to practise, it may be helpful to initially choose a couple of ideas from this list and adjust and build on them as you deepen your self-love practice. Notice how you feel when you start to implement some. Maybe keep a journal to jot down any changes you notice. Remember, baby steps build to big steps eventually and remaining consistent on this journey will help you longer term.

Self-love flowchart

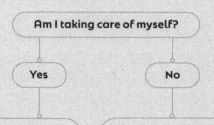

Am I taking care of myself?

Yes   No

Congratulations.

Celebrate you and keep doing what you're doing.

Step 1: Ask yourself, 'What do I need right now?'

This step is a crucial part of self-love and enables you to check-in with yourself to start the process of meeting your needs. This could be rest, or to move your body, to take some deep breaths, or connection.

Step 2: Now ask yourself, 'What actions do I need to take to meet these needs?'

For example, if you're feeling tired, you may want to create some space in your day to factor in some rest or book some time off work. If you're feeling lonely, you could text a friend or arrange a meet-up. Or if you're feeling stressed, it could be as simple as taking a pause and journalling out your feelings or writing a self-care to-do list. And if it's a more challenging act of self-love, where you recognise you want to start breaking unhealthy habits, then you may start to create a plan to work on this. Remember that self-love can also involve reaching out to others. Self-love doesn't have to be a journey on your own.

Step 3: Implement the plan.

Make small promises to yourself based on the above. And if it feels too challenging, focus on the next small step in front of you. One step at a time, just that. And remember to include compassion and kindness to yourself.

Step 4: Reflection.

Think, 'How did I feel after working through and implementing these steps?'

If better, then notice what you've learned about self-love and use this tool when next needed, and remind yourself that self-love is an ongoing process and the more you do, the more you will feel better about yourself and the less likely your needs will be left unmet.

If you still feel like there is room for growth, then go back to Step 1. Could you do something differently based on what you've learned during this process? Deep self-love can be challenging so be gentle with yourself through these steps.

The healthy choice of self-love

By taking care of yourself from the perspective of self-love, you can learn to make healthier choices. For example, if you notice that you spend too much time scrolling on social media, you can put in a self-boundary by limiting the time you spend scrolling and choosing to go out for a walk instead. You could also ask yourself some gentle questions around why you reach for your phone. What does the act of social media scrolling give you? Escapism? You might notice that you are feeling overwhelmed by a situation, so start to incorporate some meditation to quieten down your mind or journal your thoughts. This enables you to feel calmer and get curious about why you became so overwhelmed and encourages you to take action to prevent overwhelm reoccurring. Self-love.

Without self-love, you may find yourself talking to yourself unkindly, getting caught up in comparison, struggling to forgive your past mistakes, not processing your emotions, not considering yourself worthy and not valuing yourself. Introducing active self-love, such as self-forgiveness, setting boundaries, engaging in self-care, practising meditation, celebrating achievements and practising gratitude, moves you towards building yourself up instead of tearing yourself down. It can help facilitate you from feeling stuck and create room for you to work on being on your own side. I'm conscious that I brought the word 'work' in there and I just want to add here that self-love doesn't happen miraculously overnight. It is a journey of exploration, of understanding and of coming back to one's self in a beautifully questioning way so that we can meet ourselves with love in the same way we meet those who truly matter to us with love.

Self-love is the foundation for building a healthy life for yourself and for those around you. When you show up for yourself in a kind and compassionate way, you pave the way to show up more wholly for others too. You can become more understanding of what it means to be a compassionate human on a deeply personal level. It is then that your relationship with both yourself and with others can flourish. Self-awareness around your needs, specifically your unmet needs within a relationship, enables you to communicate how your needs are not being met.

By creating space for self-love as a way of living, you can build your resilience. When life throws you a knockback, such as a relationship ending or a struggle with chronic illness, the continued practice of self-love can help you have access to the resources within to offer yourself compassion and recognise the areas for growth and learning. The healthier choices that self-love encourages overall, for both our physical and mental wellbeing, lead us to feel happier and more content. Acts of self-love, such as resting when tired, reaching out when needing help, offering kind words when stressed and treating yourself as you would treat someone you care about, lead us to more contentment and less angst. And when you feel good about yourself, you see the world a little differently. The world seen through a lens of self-love is more beautiful.

Ten ways to practise self-love

1. Write down your feelings.

2. Review and refresh your boundaries.

3. Surround yourself with people who lift you up.

4. Incorporate movement into your day.

5. Schedule time for joy.

6. Give yourself a compliment.

7. Buy yourself flowers.

8. Check-in with yourself.

9. Cook a glorious new recipe.

10. Speak to yourself kindly.

Notice how your body responds to these practices. What sensations do you feel? Connect with the feeling inside. This is the magic ingredient of self-love. This is where the benefit of the deep inner practice happens and the more we commit to this self-practice, the more our mind and body can respond in positive ways. Trust.

Journal prompts for self-love

- What are some self-limiting beliefs that you would like to work on?

- What areas of your life would you like to make changes to?

- What are three compliments you could give yourself? If you find this hard, can you explore where those messages are coming from?

- What are the things and who are the people that energise you?

- What are the things and who are the people that drain you?

- What boundaries do you feel you need to put in place?

- What's something in your life that you would like to let go of?

- What is something you would like to forgive yourself for?

- What would help you feel more content?

- How can you give yourself a break?

- What is one thing you can do today for your mind, your body and your soul?

- What things are you grateful for?

- How can you love yourself a little more?

Keep nourishing yourself with love, kindness, compassion, patience and understanding and watch how you grow, bloom and evolve. Learn to meet yourself where you are instead of fighting yourself for not being enough. See how self-love moves you to a different dance, one of gentleness, trust and acceptance. Embody this. Keep nurturing yourself with self-love.

Chapter Four

On Being Authentic

The beauty of coming home to your authentic self can show up as:

- a deeper inner knowing of who you are.

- deeper connections with others.

- not hiding yourself.

- embracing your vulnerability.

- owning who you are.

- shining brightly.

- living a life that feels aligned.

- a deep inner contentment.

- improved mental wellbeing.

- trusting your inner wisdom.

- being who you were always meant to be.

Embracing authenticity

Authenticity is the presence of a genuine connection to your true self.. When we live in a place of authenticity, we live in alignment with our core values and beliefs, and free ourselves from other people's expectations of who they think we should be. Authenticity requires self-awareness, emotional maturity and self-honesty.

definition

If we think of authenticity as the deep inner knowing of who we are, that connection to ourselves that feels true and aligned, then this is the essence of coming back home to ourselves. That feeling when we take a deep, soul-nourishing breath and, in the exhale, come back home to us. It's a 'Yes that's me, I'm here.' A deep inner knowing.

Maybe you'd like to try it now. If it feels safe to do so, place one hand on your heart and one on your belly. Take a beautiful inhalation in, hold for a count of 1 at the top and then exhale slowly, noticing any sensations as you breathe out. Now take one more. Did you feel it? A shoulder-dropping, relaxing, inward-connecting moment back to yourself, to your core?

Authenticity is about coming back to yourself in the moment. It's about meeting your real, transparent and true self, free from pretending to be someone else, wearing a mask or people pleasing.

You are always here, just one breath away from coming back to your authentic connection to self: home.

In this chapter, you will gain a deeper understanding of the layers of authenticity, and I will encourage you to come back to your true self, tapping into your intuition and inner wisdom as valuable information to help guide you back home.

I encourage you to embrace your true self, free from expectations, societal pressures and removed from the concerns of the opinions of others. Authenticity is not about perfection; it's about self-awareness, self-acceptance and seeking understanding of who you are at your core. It's about showing up in all your humanness and not as a moulded version of yourself that you think everyone else will accept. This takes courage. You may face rejection or judgement, but by doing this, you can have a deeper, more authentic connection with others, where you no longer have to pretend to be anyone other than yourself. You will embrace the uniqueness of yourself. You will come home to who you are and not who you feel you should be.

Have you ever been in a room full of people, not knowing who you should be or how you should act? And then you've found yourself pretending to be someone you're not just to fit in? Have those interactions left you feeling uneasy? You didn't feel safe to be your authentic self. You didn't feel at home within yourself or amongst others in the room.

Now consider a time when you felt comfortable to talk endlessly. You felt safe to be yourself, embracing your uniqueness, taking up space. It feels different, doesn't it? Connections you make when you come from this place can leave you feeling more at ease, happier within yourself and more at home. When comfortable, your nervous system comes out of its stress response of fight/flight/freeze/fawn and into safety. We'll learn more about our nervous system in Chapter Five.

Showing up from a place of inauthenticity can lead to situations that make you feel uncomfortable. It may cause you to feel stressed or anxious, which may manifest as irritability, tension and frustration. The constant effort to maintain an image to fit in can leave you feeling mentally exhausted. All these feelings may activate our nervous system to enter our fight/flight/freeze/fawn response.

Vulnerability is the willingness to show our true selves to others and to ourselves. It's deep self-honesty about our thoughts, emotions and feelings. It's an opening up of ourselves for others to see. It can leave us feeling self-conscious as it can take us away from feeling safe. Vulnerability differs from authenticity as it refers to the willingness to be open and exposed with others whereas authenticity is about being true to oneself.

definition

Authenticity can be challenging to achieve if you have spent years conforming and trying to be someone you're not. You may struggle to embrace vulnerability, or step outside other people's expectations of you. Coming back home to yourself will enable you to embark on a journey where you feel safe to be your true self. Showing up authentically, from a place that feels like home, can lead to more beautiful and flourishing connections than inauthenticity will ever bring.

How to come back home to yourself

Coming back home to yourself is about embracing who you truly are, noticing and accepting your unique qualities, strengths, imperfections and vulnerabilities. It's about a deep inner honouring of yourself. About recognising the courage it takes to live a life that makes sense to you, instead of what someone else envisages your life should look like. It requires you to gently unmask the layers, own your story, embrace vulnerability, cultivate self-compassion, seek authentic connections, overcome resistance and choose authenticity moving forward.

Take a moment to ask yourself whether you feel fulfilled right now. Are you showing up as the best version of you? Do you feel content in the places you spend your day? Now imagine what feeling fulfilled would look and feel like? What does the best version of you showing up look like? How would you like to spend your days? Do you see differences? Take a moment here to journal about your thoughts and come back to this section to explore further.

The reasons why you may struggle to show up as your authentic self are wrapped in societal pressures, cultural expectations, past traumas and lived experiences. And each of these may have an impact on the choices you've made in your life that have left you feeling disconnected from your true self. Imagine someone who grew up wanting to be a singer but was encouraged by their family to pursue a career as a doctor. By doing so, they went against their core aspirations. They experience internal conflict and induced stress, as they attempt to navigate a life that feels out of alignment with their true self. This could manifest as frustration, unhappiness, dissatisfaction and emotional stress, and is an example of both societal pressures and cultural expectations taking someone away from feeling at home in themselves.

Alignment refers to living a life that feels gloriously harmoniously balanced. It's the process of living from a place of continued self-reflection and self-growth so that your thoughts, beliefs, emotions, values, actions and goals support you to live a life that feels fulfilled and authentic to you.

definition

Some may engage in people-pleasing behaviours, often caused by a fear of rejection or judgement from others if they express their true thoughts, emotions or needs. Have you ever been in a situation where you found yourself agreeing with others' opinions, even when it's not what you really feel? Maybe you didn't feel safe to express your own thoughts or didn't consider your view to be of value? So many of us have experienced this. But in doing so, we have suppressed our own authentic voice and undermined our sense of self. If you do this, you may feel out of alignment with yourself, which can lead to feeling frustrated and uncomfortable, as you show up as a version of yourself that is not who you want to be. But imagine another scenario where you feel safe to voice your thoughts and emotions. Can you feel the connection back to self here?

When you imagine being in spaces where you feel comfortable to show up as yourself, do you feel a sense of coming back home to yourself?

If you've experienced trauma, you may put up walls to protect yourself from ever experiencing pain or hurt again. Yet by doing so, you may find yourself avoiding certain emotions or situations that may trigger memories, for example, not allowing yourself to fall in love again as past relationships caused such hurt. Or maybe you experience constant worry or fear about being hurt again, causing everything around you to feel potentially dangerous so you socially withdraw and, as a result, feel lonely. And whilst these feelings are completely understandable, you are living a life that can leave you feeling disconnected from your true self. You deserve to feel love, to be loved and to give love. You deserve to trust and be trusted. The layers of protection you create are not enabling you to be able to connect to both yourself and to others. They are not allowing you to flourish as your authentic self. Instead, you may be living in a constant state of survival (in fight/flight/freeze/fawn mode). Living inauthentically.

I hope that some of the words here help you come back to a place that feels more like home. This act of peeling back the layers and offering ourselves understanding to why we may not be living a life that feels authentic is the starting point of coming back home. Let me help guide you to find a way.

2. OWNING YOUR STORY

Owning your story is a transformative part of coming home to self. It requires you to reach a place of acceptance, and this can be reached by offering yourself the understanding that what you uncovered in the peeling back of layers does not define you. It is the roots for you to grow and to shape your future without the need to hide or be ashamed of your experiences. An important step here is self-compassion. Self-compassion is the antidote to shame. And stories and experiences shared in safe spaces can help reduce the tight grip shame may have on you. It helps validate your experiences. It can affirm that your feelings, thoughts and emotions are deserving of attention and understanding. It can help you feel seen, heard and accepted. It can help you feel less alone, and this in itself can help you move out of a stress response and back into connection with yourself. It can be so healing.

Can you recall a time you shared something you were struggling with emotionally that was met with compassion? Did you notice the emotional stress you had been suppressing alleviate? Maybe you offered yourself understanding words in the moment, instead of judgement, and felt yourself breathe a little more deeply. These are important steps when coming out of a stress response and back into connection and home with self. You may begin to notice the tiny shifts, the moments where healing felt possible and connection to self felt reachable. Noticing these shifts, however tiny, may help you see that movement out of the stress response (that inauthenticity can leave us in) is a possibility.

When you own that you are struggling with your mental health and choose to share your experiences more openly, you help to break the stigma around it. Not only do you show up for yourself from a place that is authentic and connected to self, but you also pave the way for others to be inspired to be able to explore their journey and struggles too. I encourage you to only explore your own story in compassionate and safe spaces until you feel at a place where you are happy to outwardly own your story. A 'me, too' culture that builds connection through shared experiences, vulnerability and courage helps contribute to a more compassionate and understanding society. It fosters a collective coming home to self instead of pretence and mask wearing.

3. OVERCOMING THE RESISTANCE

Another key step in coming home to yourself is gently exploring the resistance to showing up authentically and understanding the reasons why you are stopping yourself from showing up in this way. We so often fear rejection, judgement and the unknown. And this can be due to our past experiences as well as our innate human blueprint for a longing to fit in, to belong and to connect. Can you meet yourself here to gently explore under the surface of this resistance? Whose messages are you listening to? Can you challenge your fears? Reframe any limiting beliefs? What small steps can you take for yourself that feel safe to come back to a life that feels more aligned for you?

Perhaps this could mean listening inwards before saying yes to someone and considering whether you really want to do what they've asked. Or maybe it could be speaking up for yourself when something feels wrong for you. Or perhaps sharing what you would like to share on social media in your own voice that speaks to you as opposed to what you feel you should be posting but feels misaligned. Another example could be limiting time with people where you don't feel yourself and spending more time in spaces where you feel valued. Take a moment to reflect on these examples and notice if these feel safe or uncomfortable to do. Very often the deeper exploring of the uncomfortableness can illuminate for us the more focused self-work that may be needed.

4. CHOOSING AN AUTHENTIC PATH

Cultivating a life that feels more authentic, that brings you back into alignment, and accepting yourself require you to choose authenticity over inauthenticity. It requires a self-responsibility that says, 'I'm on my own side.' It leads you to living a life not limited by societal expectations. It gives you a voice. One way to cultivate a deeper understanding of yourself here moving forward is to write your name on a piece of paper and reflect on what your name means to you. Who is this person? What are their values? What matters to them? What do you want for them? What is holding them back? Who is the person behind the name? This deeply creative, experiential exploration can help move us to being at the centre of our world and not just a small part in it. It can help cultivate a returning home to self.

Through these steps, you can start moving towards embracing and nurturing authenticity to feel more at home within yourself. It takes courage to break free from old patterns of behaviour, where you aren't being authentic, such as people pleasing, mask-wearing or showing up in places where you can't be your true self, but the rewards are huge. How would it feel to show up as yourself, where you feel accepted, valued and seen by those around you? How would it feel to live a safer, more aligned life? Do you want a life where you've embraced your own passions and not followed someone else's dream? Authenticity is hard, but it's the journey home.

Listening to your inner wisdom

Inner wisdom is your innate inner guidance and deep inner knowledge that enables you to give meaning to your experiences, to question your thoughts, challenge your belief system and offer yourself your truth.

definition

Inner wisdom is the core within yourself that guides you home. It is your unique internal compass that offers clarity based on your lived experiences, moments and understanding of the world around you. It is an incredibly powerful, personal resource that will gently guide you if you take the time to listen.

In our busy lives, many of us fall into a habit of not listening inwards. It can be hard to embrace and to get in touch with our inner wisdom. One way to help connect to it is through quietening down the outside noise and engaging in self-reflection and mindfulness. Activities such as journalling, meditation and bringing your attention back to the present moment by taking in your surroundings and breathing deeply (What can you see? What can you hear?) can be useful ways to do this. Even taking a moment to check-in with yourself and asking, 'How am I in this moment and what do I need?' These practices are key components of connecting to our authenticity as we can use them to connect with the core of ourselves and connect with what feels safe and aligned as opposed to what evokes a stress response.

The feeling that something is not right, our gut feeling that has us questioning whether we want to trust something or not, occurs almost instinctively. This is your intuition.

> **Intuition**, when viewed in the context of your nervous system, is your awareness of safety and threat. It is automatic and happens before your thinking mind engages and gives the intuition meaning (our inner wisdom). Intuition brings physiological changes, such as increased heart rate, impulses, change in tone of voice, stomach pain and feelings of nervousness.

definition

Have you ever felt something is off when you enter a room? There's little time for us to listen inwards as our intuition kicks in almost impulsively. When we have an instant feeling inside that something isn't right, it is our intuition speaking to us. It is our nervous system searching for cues of safety. Remember: the primary function of our nervous system is to keep us safe (we'll talk about this more in the next chapter).

Whilst intuition is an immediate nervous system response, your inner wisdom is a deeper knowledge that comes from a connection to yourself. It enables us to probe a little deeper and challenge the initial intuition. Inner wisdom is your inner parent. It's reassuring, it's balanced, it asks questions, it may challenge the intuition a little, getting in touch with your vulnerability, whilst also offering reassurance and validation for feeling a certain way. Let's return to feeling something is 'off' in the room you've just walked in to. Maybe you feel unsafe in the room? Perhaps your connections to others in the room are inauthentic? Maybe you feel you have to wear a mask? You can't be yourself. You don't feel at home.

Your intuition picks up initial cues from the room, and you may experience an increase in heart rate, shortness of breath, sweating and less of a connection with yourself than how you feel 'at home'. Your inner wisdom gives these feelings meaning:

'I don't feel supported here', 'I don't share the same values as these people', 'Hang on, is this me making up stories?' or 'I'm exhausted and would rather be at home right now.' By listening to your inner wisdom, you can start to make informed choices about who you spend time with based on how they make you feel inside. You can challenge your intuition and reflect on why you may not feel like your true self in the room.

Let's consider another example. Maybe you're thinking about a career change because although you currently have a good job that offers security, something feels like it is missing. This is our intuition. And then, when you reflect on the feeling and bring awareness in, you notice that the job isn't aligning with your passions. This is your inner wisdom stepping in. And even though to change jobs can bring uncertainty, your intuition keeps nudging you that way and your inner wisdom can help bring scenarios and options to consider. Embracing our inner wisdom helps us move forward to living a more fulfilling life. And although career moves may not be an option for everyone, even bringing in small elements of change can bring fulfilment. Maybe you work in a bank but would love to work in floristry, so you start attending more floristry workshops at the weekend. It's the tiny steps of change that plant the seeds for growth and new ideas to bloom that feel more aligned and connected to that sense of feeling at home.

Life is a process of tiny steps, of growing awareness, of ideas evolving and blooming.

> **Felt sense** refers to the subtle bodily sensations that arise in our awareness when we try to understand or give meaning to a situation. It's the body's way of listening for inner cues that provide non-verbal implicit meanings that make sense for us. For example, if the sensations reveal unease, it may mean that something doesn't align, yet feelings of lightness, ease or excitement may reveal that something seems right. The felt sense can differ from your inner wisdom as the sensations may not always fit with the inner wisdom, so it's a process of trying on different conscious thoughts for that inner wisdom to meet the sensations in unity.
>
> *definition*

When we start to listen inwards, we can hear our own voice come through. It may take some time to connect with this voice, and you may find it hard to hear your own wisdom if you've spent a lifetime listening and embodying others' opinions and values, which haven't been healthy for you. But with practice, we can work towards releasing the holds that maybe have us in their grip, such as family pressures, societal and cultural norms as well as social media consumption messages that may be influencing us and conflicting with our authentic self. It takes courage to step away from these pressures and being authentic isn't easy. But with gentleness and questioning, it can help you reach a place that feels more in alignment with your true self longer term. Think small changes rather than drastic ones as these will be easier to maintain going forward.

Your inner wisdom will look different from everyone else's. The life you've lived and the lens through which you see life will both contribute here, but taking time to connect with your inner wisdom can be a grounding experience that brings you closer to meeting yourself. It will help guide you forward in a way that is more aligned with yourself. Noticing with each step how your body responds and what happens next, to find a way to listen with curiosity rather than fear, can help create a shift within. And it's the noticing of these shifts, such as a deeper inhalation of breath, a relaxing of the muscles or an ensuing slight ease within, that can help guide you forward to a path that feels more you. Let's look at the following exercise for listening inwards, based on Gendlin's Focusing Technique.

Tune in to your inner wisdom

Step 1: Clearing a space

Find a quiet and comfortable place where you can sit and just be with yourself for a few moments. Take in some deep breaths and allow yourself to relax and become really present. This is an important step, so take a moment to let yourself feel calm and relaxed. Quieten down the outside noise and centre yourself in this moment.

Step 2: Identifying a felt sense

A felt sense is a bodily awareness that is full of information about your inner experience. It's the sensations felt within. It can be hard to connect with this felt sense at first as it's not always obvious. Think of it as a process of listening inwards. So, focus on the specific issue that you're feeling stuck on and want some inner answers on. How is your body reacting when you focus on the issue? Ease? Discomfort? Rapid breathing? Or deeper breathing? Sweating? Tense? This is a body sense of the issue. What information/awareness is there? It's normal for this to feel unclear and murky at first.

Step 3: Getting a handle on the felt sense

Describe the felt sense in words or images. This might not feel clear at first. That's OK. It's a normal reaction at this stage. Expect lots of 'Erm, I don't know', 'Just a feeling'. Keep digging a little deeper, connecting even more to the sense until you feel a quality of the felt sense that fits right. It might be a word like stuck, heavy, blurry. Or an image of dark or light.

Step 4: Resonating

Use this step to check-in with the word or image from Step 3. How does it resonate? Does it fit? Allow the felt sense to settle and the image or word to take a deeper hold to really capture the essence of the sense.

Step 5: Asking

Ask yourself, 'What is this sense trying to tell me?' Stay with the felt sense until you feel a shift in your body. When something connects and feels right, our nervous system responds in a way that feels more at ease. The answer is in this shift. If an answer comes in without feeling the shift, let it go and ask again. The shift is key. It's a slight release or a slight 'give' in tension. Explore deeper here.

Step 6: Receiving

Allow yourself to consider the answer from Step 5. Let it settle and sit. You may experience more shifts as things become clearer to help you move from feeling stuck with the issue. Repeat these steps to allow more answers to come in.

Journal prompts for coming home to yourself

- What does coming home to yourself mean to you?

- How does it feel? What three words would you use to describe that feeling?

- What are the things that make you feel most you? Describe that feeling? Where do you feel it in your body? How can you create space to do more of them?

- Who are the people that make you feel most you and why?

- What are the things that don't align in your life and that drain you? What are the ways you could set boundaries around these?

- What are the things that are stopping you be who you want to be? How can you remove these barriers?

- How can you cultivate a healthier relationship with yourself in terms of meeting your needs, the way you view yourself and incorporating more self-compassion and kindness?

- How can you open space to be more deeply honest with yourself and listen to your inner wisdom?

- What is your inner wisdom saying? How can you create time to listen inwards more?

- What three words could you use to describe your inner core self?

- What is a promise to yourself you could make today to connect a little deeper to yourself going forward?

It's not the world who needs you to show up as your beautiful authentic self, it's you who needs you to.

Chapter Five

On Finding Calm

Things that you may not realise are disrupting your inner calm are:

- internalising other people's opinions of you.

- saying yes when you mean no.

- allowing your negative thoughts to spiral.

- not healing from past traumas.

- engaging in mindless scrolling.

- spending time with people who don't support you.

- not getting enough sleep.

- engaging in self-sabotaging behaviours.

- not reaching out for help.

- not choosing you.

Amidst the hustle and bustle of our daily lives, we can often find ourselves facing situations that can unsettle our sense of calm. Life's demands can stir up a sense of what feels like unease in our nervous system at times. This is normal. And this chapter is a gentle exploration of how we can navigate life's challenges with tenderness, so that we restore a sense of serenity in our days, guiding you through ways to connect a little more deeply with your nervous system to help you bring healthy regulation.

Nervous system regulation refers to the ability to healthily bring the nervous system back to a sense of safety (connection) after experiencing a fight/flight/freeze/fawn response (activation of protective states), so that we no longer feel overwhelmed (and come back to a sense of connection with ourselves). A regulated nervous system has the capacity to hold many different emotions.

definition

Understanding your nervous system

Think of those mornings when your alarm clock startles you awake, setting off a chain reaction of stress as you rush to get ready for work, battling the clock. Consider the moments when you're in a difficult meeting at work, maybe your heart races and your palms feel sweaty. Or maybe you're sat in gridlocked traffic and you're running late for something. The everyday situations, such as looming deadlines, an unexpected bill or the worry of poor health, can all cause our nervous system to feel 'switched on'.

But it's not just external circumstances that can send ripples of unease through our nervous system. Interactions with the people in our lives play a significant role as well. Think about a disagreement with a friend where words are exchanged in the heat of the moment, leaving your heart pounding and your mind racing. Or consider the heartache that can arise from difficult family relationships where unresolved tensions sit within the background of the relationship, simmering away and causing continued unease. And then, there are the complexities of romantic relationships, such as issues within the relationship or the longing for a relationship. These relational turmoils can trigger emotional imbalance and hugely affect our sense of calm. They can manifest as activation of our fight/flight/freeze/fawn response (our natural protective states) and, of course, differ for each of us depending on our lived experiences of how we are able to handle the ups and downs of life. A certain amount of activation is normal and healthy as our body searches for cues of safety but it's when this activation becomes chronic or impacts our daily living that it may require some more attention and support. This is known as dysregulation.

Dysregulation. Have you ever felt like your nervous system is out of sync and feeling off-balance and activated? This is dysregulation and can present as two distinct manifestations. One is hyperarousal, where you might feel constantly on edge, restless and anxious. The other is hypoarousal, which can make you feel lethargic, demotivated and disconnected from yourself and, in more extreme cases, numb and dissociated.

definition

In Chapter One, we learned how our nervous system is an intricate network that connects our mind and body, and how it affects the way we feel and communicate with the environment around us. In Chapter Two, we looked at how our attachment style can also play a part in our ability to healthily regulate our nervous system. To recap, if you are anxiously attached, you may experience feelings of insecurity and worry that your partner may leave you. On the other hand, someone with an avoidant attachment style may hide their feelings. Both can lead to some long-term activation in the nervous system that feels like unease. And this unease may manifest as some restlessness and feeling on edge if anxiously attached or disconnected from feelings and feeling numb if avoidant attached. Both examples lead us away from a feeling of a deeper sense of calm (connection) within our nervous system.

It's very true that an activated nervous system can present in different ways. Maybe you've felt those feelings of restlessness and worry. Or irritability, where you feel more easily agitated. Or feeling on guard, finding it difficult to concentrate and even feeling mood swings. But activation can also cause physical symptoms, such as headaches, stomach pains and difficulty sleeping. And this is because our nervous system is intricately connected to our body via our vagus nerve. These physical symptoms can, of course, vary in intensity and duration depending on the situation and the personal circumstances. The important thing is to become more self-aware around your nervous system, so that you can detect when it's feeling symptoms of unease (our fight/flight/freeze/fawn protective states) and use tools (some of which are offered later in this chapter) to bring about healthy regulation and a sense of being back in control, which feels like connection back to self.

A gentle note for you: Prolonged nervous system dysregulation can be exhausting and often hints at a deeper level of work needed. Life experiences such as chronic stress, unhealed trauma, mental health issues, chronic illness, lack of social support, unresolved past issues, prolonged grief or loss can play a huge part in long-term dysregulation. These experiences can be hugely isolating and often frightening to handle alone. Please know that you don't have to struggle in isolation. If you notice that tools are not working, and you are remaining in a state of dysregulation, then please reach out to someone you trust. Finding a way to feel calm within your nervous system is an act of self-love and deep self-care. With the right help, you will be able to move towards feeling safer within your body. Something that we all deserve.

Befriending your nervous system and finding healthy regulation

I remember the first time I learned how to befriend my nervous system and feeling like it was this unlocking of a hidden sanctuary within that I could learn to access at any time to bring not only feelings of peace to my thoughts but a feeling of deep calm to my body. Pure magic.

It enabled me to gain a sense of control over my emotional responses instead of them controlling me. Through connecting with the way my nervous system was responding, giving meaning and understanding to my reactions, then using tools to soothe, I could come back to a place that felt easier to be in. I want to show you how you can do this, too, so that you can find your way back to a place that feels safer and calmer.

When we befriend our nervous system and learn how to bring healthy regulation, everyday stressful situations become more manageable:

- Imagine the weight of your worries gently lifting with every breath, creating space for a deep sense of inner calm.

- Imagine the weight of past anxieties and regrets slowly dissipating as you open up room for healing.

- Imagine the weight of emotional overwhelm lessening as you meet yourself with self-compassion and understanding.

- Imagine the weight of blame melting away as you embrace self-forgiveness and accept your humanness.

- Imagine the weight of a stressful situation becoming easier to cope with as you find ways to bring self-compassion.

- Imagine the weight of uncertainty and fear releasing as you create space for courage and resilience.

- Imagine the weight of prolonged dysregulation being replaced with gentle nervous system regulation through patience, understanding and healing.

How did you feel reading these? Did you feel hope? Maybe you felt there was possibility for feeling the release of this weight. These are all examples of healthy nervous system regulation. Having the skills to handle this is the essence of living a balanced life with ease.

EXERCISE

Befriend your nervous system

1. Notice that your body is experiencing a stress response of fight/flight/freeze/fawn (protective state).

2. Acknowledge the stress response and remind yourself that it's your body doing its best to protect you.

3. Give meaning to why the stress response may be there (maybe it is occurring due to a confrontation with a friend or ahead of a big meeting at work).

Choose a self-regulation tool (examples in next section), so that you can be with the stress response and not in it.

5. Repeat as necessary until you can approach the situation from a place that feels easier to be in (from a place of connection with self).

How regulated is your nervous system currently?

1. On a typical day, how often do you find yourself feeling over-whelmed by stress or anxiety?

   a. I rarely feel stressed or anxious.

   b. I occasionally do but can manage it.

   c. I often feel stressed and overwhelmed.

   d. It feels like I'm constantly stressed and anxious.

2. When faced with a challenging situation, how do you usually react?

   a. I stay calm and composed.

   b. I become slightly anxious but can manage it.

   c. I often feel stressed.

   d. I almost always feel intense anxiety or completely withdraw.

3. How do you generally handle unexpected changes to plans that you had?

   a. I'm not fazed by changes.

   b. I manage but wish that they hadn't been changed.

   c. I struggle but do eventually adapt.

   d. I feel significantly distressed and either become visibly emotional or very withdrawn.

4. How do you respond to constructive criticism?

   a. I see it as an opportunity to grow.

   b. My first reaction is to get defensive but then I see it as a way to help me.

   c. I find it difficult to accept.

   d. I react with strong defensiveness and emotional outbursts.

5. When having a challenging conversation, how do you typically respond?

   a. I remain calm, listen to understand and respond empathically.

   b. I can become emotional but still effectively communicate.

   c. I can become very emotional, which makes communication difficult.

   d. I always become very emotional or very quiet and communication is impossible.

6. How well do you manage your workload?

   a. Very well.

   b. Mostly well.

   c. I find it difficult and often struggle.

   d. I'm completely overwhelmed, visibly stressed and emotionally dysregulated.

7. How do you react to conflict and disagreement with others?

   a. I remain calm and look to understand and seek resolution.

   b. I look for resolution but can feel emotional.

   c. I often feel distressed and struggle to remain calm.

   d. I frequently experience an intense emotional reaction or become very withdrawn.

8. When you find yourself running late for an appointment, how do you typically react?

   a. I remain calm and do my best to arrive on time, knowing that getting stressed will not help the situation.

   b. I feel anxious.

   c. I feel very stressed and struggle to manage my time generally.

   d. I'm always running late, and I'm always greatly emotionally dysregulated by it.

9. When you have free time do you find it easy to switch off and relax?

   a. I can always switch off.

   b. I can switch off most of the time.

   c. Only occasionally. I can often feel guilty for resting.

   d. I rarely switch off.

10. How is your sleep?

   a. I fall asleep easily and wake up feeling refreshed.

   b. My sleep is mostly OK but sometimes I may struggle to fall asleep.

   c. I often struggle to sleep or wake up frequently through the night.

   d. My sleep is awful. I really struggle and often lie awake.

RESULTS

- Mostly As: Your nervous system appears to be well-regulated, and you can handle life's ups and downs with calmness and ease.

- Mostly Bs: Your nervous system is moderately regulated but may benefit from some additional techniques (see following section).

- Mostly Cs: Your nervous system may need some help in healthy regulation as you can be greatly impacted by stress.

- Mostly Ds: Your nervous system appears to be dysregulated and it may benefit from some more professional help with finding ways to healthily regulate it.

These questions serve as a gentle guide for you to see how your nervous system reacts in general to life's everyday stressors. And it's important to note that each situation may get a different response on a different day but if you feel after answering these questions that you'd like to feel calmer and approach life's ups and downs in a more grounded way, then please know that help is available. As mentioned in the previous section, if you consider you are stuck in a dysregulated state, there may be other factors that require some more professional help. You don't have to continue living life in such a dysregulated way, which (as highlighted in Chapter One) can lead to chronic stress and poor mental health.

Building a self-care toolkit

I love the concept of a self-care toolkit as it enables you to build a personalised collection of activities that you can call upon when needed to support the healthy regulation of your nervous system. The key is remembering to use them during times of stress and emotional turmoil to prevent the nervous system becoming more and more dysregulated.

Whilst it's a common belief that our fight/flight/freeze/fawn response is essential for our safety, the truth is that we are at our safest when our nervous system returns to a calmer state. It's from this state that we can make more rational decisions as our executive functions of our brain (the pre-frontal cortex) come back online. Consider the difference in your reactions when you've been angry in the past or upset and how you've viewed the situation once you've calmed down. This isn't to say that we should ignore the reasons for our anger or emotions that our body is trying to communicate with us (as discussed in Chapter One), but rather to understand that having the tools to help maintain emotional regulation, which helps us make clearer, more rational decisions, is vital for our overall mental wellbeing.

To help with this, I'm sharing some tools below that use a combination of practices combining the breath, body and mind to bring about healthy self-regulation. I find it useful to choose two or three from each section to pop into my own personal toolkit that I can access when needed. Maybe you could choose some from each list for your own toolkit. It can be helpful to meet a stress response with an exercise that aligns with the intensity of the stress. For instance, during a fight/flight stress response, engaging in some slow, gentle breathing might not be as effective as an initial deep breath in and forceful exhalation. Alternatively, a gentle tapping exercise may not be as impactful as energetically dancing to release any stored tension. On the other hand, a freeze response may be better managed with gentle breathing rather than a brisk walk or run. A helpful tip is to meet the stress response where it currently is. Imagine feeling stressed and sharing your feelings with someone – if they respond with a very calm 'Why don't you just relax!', it may not be as helpful as if they matched your energy by saying, 'I totally get that!' Similarly, when we're feeling down, hearing someone say, 'Oh come on, it will be OK,' with high energy might not be as comforting as them gently asking, 'Is there anything I can do to help?' Having others meet us at our own energy level allows our nervous system to begin calming down, as we feel acknowledged and understood. Conversely, not feeling understood can lead to increased activation and stress.

USING YOUR BREATH TO REGULATE YOUR NERVOUS SYSTEM

Deep breathing exercises help activate the calming receptors in our nervous system (the parasympathetic path). By consciously slowing and deepening our breath, we send messages to our body that it's safe. This, in turn, can help reduce stress responses in the body.

1. **The candle breath:** Breathe in through your nose for a count of 4, hold for a count of 1 and then exhale through your mouth as if you were blowing a candle out hard.

2. **The 4, 7, 8 breath:** Breathe in through your nose for a count of 4, hold for a count of 7 and then exhale slowly through your mouth for a count of 8.

3. **The deep belly/soul nourishing breath:** Take a deep breath in slowly through your nose, feeling your belly expand. Hold for a few seconds, and then exhale slowly through your mouth, feeling your belly empty of air.

4. **The box breath:** Breathe in through your nose for a count of 4, hold for a count of 4, exhale through your mouth for a count of 4, hold for a count of 4. As you breathe, then hold, visualise the side of a square.

5. **The alternate nostril breath:** Place your right thumb over your right nostril and inhale through your left nostril. At the top of the inhale, place your right finger over your left nostril and exhale through your right nostril. Inhale through your right nostril, at the top, place your right thumb over your right nostril and exhale through your left.

6. **The Dirga Pranayama breath (three-part breath):** Take a deep breath into your belly, feeling it fill your upper chest and then your throat. Exhale feeling the breath release from your throat, your upper chest and then your belly.

Find one of these breathing exercises that you like the most and repeat a few cycles of them. If at any time this does not feel comfortable for you, please do not continue. Breathwork doesn't suit everyone.

USING YOUR BODY TO REGULATE YOUR NERVOUS SYSTEM

By getting out of our head and getting into our body in a conscious effort to make our body feel safer, we send cues of safety to our nervous system, which can enable us to feel calmer.

1. **Therapeutic body shaking:** Intentionally shake your body to release physical tension. Our bodies often hold on to tension and the shaking can help release it. Body shaking can be done whilst standing up, lying down or sitting. Start by taking a deep breath and then take one of your arms and shake it for 10–30 seconds and sigh out your breath. Take deep breaths in and continue to sigh them out. Now repeat the same exercise with your other arm, and then try shaking each leg. Notice how the shaking feels in your body. What emotions are easing or coming to the surface? How did your body react once you'd finished shaking?

2. **Body scan:** Follow a guided body scan online or sit or lie somewhere comfortably and bring your attention to all the different parts of your body starting from the crown of your head all the way down to the toes. Breathe in deeply and slowly exhale as you focus on each body part. Notice how your body may calm as you bring awareness to these parts.

3. **Muscle relaxation:** Find a comfortable space and start with some deep breaths to relax. Begin with your toes and work up. Tense a muscle group for 5–10 seconds, and then release and focus on the relaxation. Breathe deeply throughout. Work your way up the body and back down. Tensing and releasing. Breathing in and breathing slowly out.

4. **Gentle stretching exercises:** These can help release any stored tension. Get creative with them and move in a way that feels releasing for you. Some gentle examples include:

   a. Neck stretch: Sit or stand with your back straight and slowly tilt your head to one side, bringing your ear towards your shoulder. Hold for 15–30 seconds whilst breathing deeply. Gently return your head to an upright position, and then repeat on the other side.

   b. Upper body stretch: Interlace your fingers in front of you with your palms facing outwards. Gently straighten your arms, pushing them away from your body. Hold for 15–30 seconds whilst breathing deeply. You can also repeat this exercise with your hands behind your back.

   c. Back stretch: This can be done whilst standing or sitting. Raise your arms overhead and gently hold your left wrist with your right hand. Then lean to your right side. Hold for 15–30 seconds, and then repeat on the other side.

5. **Dancing or exercise:** Putting your favourite music on and moving your body in a way that feels good for you helps release stored tension and allows the nervous system to regulate. Or try going for a run.

6. **Tapping:** Also known as Emotional Freedom Technique (EFT), this is a process of gently tapping specific points on the body. It's a form of acupressure that may help relieve tension and bring calm. The butterfly technique shown in Chapter One is a helpful tapping practice. But you may also want to try the following short tapping exercise:

   a. Find a quiet space and get comfortable.

   b. Close your eyes and take a few deep breaths.

c. Use the tip of your fingers (usually your index and middle fingers) to gently tap specific points on your body. You may want to repeat a calming phrase to yourself whilst you do this, such as 'I am safe' or 'I am releasing all tension.' Tap 5–7 times gently on the following points, breathing deeply as you do:

  – The top of your head.

  – The edge of your eyebrow near the bridge of your nose.

  – The outer corner of your eye.

  – Under your nose.

  – Under your lower lip.

  – The centre of your chest on your heart.

  – Just below your collarbone.

  After tapping all the points, take a deep breath and exhale slowly. Notice how you feel and repeat as often as needed.

7. **Connection with others:** Connecting with those who you feel safe with is a powerful calming tool. It helps regulate the nervous system by releasing hormones that promote us to feel good such as oxytocin. Call or text a friend, hug a loved one or reach out to someone you trust.

8. **Walking in nature:** This helps regulate the nervous system as it is a deeply grounding practice. Try focusing on the sensation of your feet on the ground, the way your body moves, the sounds you hear, the scents you smell and the awe of nature you see.

9. **Soothing self-touch:** Self-touch, if this feels safe for you, can be incredibly healing and is an excellent tool for self-regulation. Try hugging yourself by placing your right hand on your upper left arm and your left hand on your upper right arm. You can also try rubbing your hands up and down your arms, tapping gently or giving each arm a light squeeze, breathing deeply

and slowly exhaling as you do. Another self-touch exercise that can be super healing is taking your hands and gently holding them on either side of your face, cupping your chin, feeling the heat of your hands against your skin. Stay here for a while and breathe deeply, noticing how your nervous system may start to calm. Notice the sensations you feel. Breathe into them.

USING YOUR MIND TO REGULATE YOUR NERVOUS SYSTEM

By consciously engaging our mind with practices such as meditation, mindfulness and journalling, we can find ways to develop more self-awareness around our emotions. Some practices that may help include:

1. **Meditation:** This practice helps lower your heart rate, which sends cues of safety to your nervous system. Research has also shown that meditation can positively boost the areas of your brain that play a part in emotional regulation. It can also improve your sleep, which is important in regulation, too. You may want to try the short 1-minute meditation in the exercise in this chapter.

2. **Journalling:** Writing out our feelings gives movement to emotions, which helps release them from being stored in the body. This practice helps with reduced tension and regulation by providing a safe space to express feelings. Try using the guided journal prompts included at the end of each chapter in this book or write down on paper what you're feeling each day or when you're particularly struggling with something.

3. **Gratitude:** The simple act of reflecting on the things that we are grateful for has such an impact on our nervous system, bringing feelings of contentment, calm and improved wellbeing. You could start by keeping a gratitude journal and take a few moments to reflect on the things you're grateful for.

A grounding exercise using mindfulness

Focus on:

> 5 things you can see.
>
> 4 things you can feel.
>
> 3 things you can hear.
>
> 2 things you can smell.
>
> 1 thing you can taste.

---

4. **Mindfulness:** Bringing our awareness back to the moment encourages us to move away from the feelings of nervous system activation and back to a connection with ourselves, and away from our fight/flight/freeze/fawn response. Take a moment to observe your breathing or observe your surroundings without judgement. One of my favourite mindfulness tools is to look out of a window and take in the scene unfolding in front of you. Maybe you notice the trees, or a bird flying past, or the way the clouds are moving, or a dog running, or a child laughing. This can help ground you back to a sense of safety.

5. **Glimmers:** Look for your glimmers. Glimmers were first coined by Deb Dana, a trauma specialist, and are best defined as the opposite of triggers. They are micro moments of awe that spark joy and evoke inner calm, which create a tiny mood shift. These shifts send cues of safety to our nervous system, which enable us to feel more at ease. Look for your own glimmers, such as:

   - Taking in a beautiful sunset.
   - The rays of sunshine on your face.
   - Listening to birdsong.
   - Receiving a random act of kindness.
   - A text from a friend.

Glimmers will look different for everyone and relate to anything tiny that brings a sense of hope, inspiration or contentment within. Notice how your glimmers make you feel. Maybe you take a deeper inhalation of breath, your shoulders drop a little, you feel yourself smile, your jaw relaxes and your mind quietens a little. All signs of activating the soothing pathways of your nervous system.

Build your own self-care toolkit

To use when needing to bring a sense of calm

Three tools using my breath:

1. _____

2. _____

3. _____

Three tools using my body:

1. _____

2. _____

3. _____

Three tools using my mind:

1. _____

2. _____

3. _____

Understanding your stress responses

The following diagrams help show you how our nervous systems can become dysregulated and how accessing regulation tools, such as the ones outlined above, can help alleviate the cycle.

UNHEALTHY STRESS RESPONSE CYCLE

Stressor/threat
(i.e. overworked)

Nervous system dysregulated:

If the behaviour continues without a check on it or a resolving of the stressor, then the next time you are faced with another stressor, you will be less able to cope and the behaviours will become less and less manageable.

Activates stress response: (fight/ flight/freeze/fawn)

Irritated with work, want to run from it, unable to engage in getting work done.

Behaviour:

(e.g. procrastination, worry or engaging in self-sabotaging behaviours, such as negative self-talk, self-doubt or even substance misuse)

You can sometimes become stuck in this stress response and these unhealthy coping strategies, so you may require more professional help.

HEALTHY STRESS RESPONSE CYCLE

Stressor/threat
(i.e. overworked)

Nervous system regulated

Activates stress response: (fight/flight/freeze/fawn)

Acknowledge that you're experiencing a stress response.

Behaviour:

Instead of engaging in unhealthy behaviours, such as self-sabotaging, you acknowledge the stress response and engage in healthy processing of the behaviours, such as regulation techniques from your self-care toolkit, or reaching out for help. Then the next time another stressor is present, you will be able to better cope with the lessons and experiences of the previous stressor as you are not stuck in survival mode.

The 1-minute meditation

Step 1: Find a comfortable space, either lying down or sitting. Close your eyes and take a deep breath in (or keep your eyes open and focus on a point in front of you if that feels more comfortable).

Step 2: Slowly inhale for the count of 4, hold for 1 at the top and then slowly exhale for the count of 5.

Step 3: Continue with this breathing and start to imagine a warm light at the top of your head. Choose a colour that feels calming to you.

Step 4: Allow this warm light to slowly scan down your body, becoming aware of the sensations as it reaches the different parts of your body.

Step 5: Notice any areas of tension, breathe into them to release and allow the light to travel from the crown of your head all the way down to your toes.

Step 6: Stay here for a while, basking in the warmth of the light. Repeat as necessary.

Journal prompts for feeling calmer

- What are three things you are grateful for?

- What sensations do you notice in your body when you practise this gratitude?

- What self-care activities make you feel most at ease?

- What are the things that bring you joy? How can you create more space for these?

- What are the things that bring you least joy? What are the ways that you can reduce these?

- What is bringing you most worry today? What is one small thing you can do to help alleviate that worry?

- What are some ways that you can be more present in your day?

- What self-care tools can you use to help feel calmer and a little more at ease?

- What is your favourite way to relax?

- What is one small thing you could add to each day to bring a moment of calmness for you?

Calmness allows us to see the beauty in the world that perhaps would otherwise have been missed. And as that inner world of calmness blooms, so do you.

Chapter Six

On Understanding Others

Maybe the world around us would be a whole lot more beautiful if we just took the time to realise that:

- everyone is going through something that they don't talk about.

- kindness could mean more than you ever realise.

- instead of thinking why would someone behave that way, we could consider what happened to them to lead them to behave a certain way.

- people's defensiveness can be hiding so much pain, shame or guilt.

- people see life through their own lens, not yours.

- everyone's life matters.

- most people are just projecting, it's not personal.

- how people show up for themselves tells you a lot about how they feel about themselves.

- we can't change people; we can only change ourselves.

- love, kindness and compassion is what helps people grow.

Understanding others

The Dictionary of Obscure Sorrows, created by John Koenig, aims to come up with new words for emotions that currently lack words. 'Sonder' is defined as the realisation that each passer-by is living a life as complex as our own. How magical is that? What a different level of emotional maturity it is to hold that word close. I most consider this word when I'm sat on the tube in London, in my own world, yet for a passing moment also present in someone else's world for the duration of my journey. Yet I'm an 'extra' in the story where they are their own main character, just as they are an extra in mine. Just for that fleeting moment. But their real life is as complex as mine, maybe even more so. The word 'sonder' helps provide a deeper level of perspective when considering others. I couldn't possibly know what news they may have heard this morning, or what they endured as a child, but I do know that chances are they are going through something that they aren't sharing, something that they are struggling with that they wish they could change. We all are, aren't we?

In the therapy room, the feeling of sonder informs much of my work. As I'm sat in front of someone as they share a story about another person they are in a relationship with and the struggles they may be having with them, I'm reminded that we can't change people (therapy isn't about coming up with solutions on how to change the people clients are struggling with). But something beautiful unfurls when we offer a perspective on why someone may behave the way they do. Of course, we can only surmise. We can't assume. But imagine if we all viewed others through the lens of what happened to them, instead of judging or blaming them? Their lens will look completely different to ours and is dependent upon their own upbringing, as well as their life experiences. And this shift in perspective can help bring compassion.

The lens through which we view the world refers to the way we see something based on our lived experiences. This influences our thoughts, feelings, the way we may interact socially and how we see the world around us.

definition

For example, some people may exhibit behaviours of defensiveness and projection. Both are psychological defence mechanisms; defensiveness is a response to protect someone's self-esteem (such as denial or not accepting blame), whilst projection is an unconscious transferring of someone's own negative thoughts or feelings on to another person. If someone lacks confidence in their appearance, they may highlight another's flaws to detract from their own insecurities. Or someone who is always late may blame everyone else for getting in their way or a train being delayed, which explains their lateness. Both responses are fear based and can be caused by many factors. Fundamentally, they may be covering up a fear of rejection, abandonment or failure. There may be a fear of being seen negatively, not being good enough, as well as a deep lack of self-worth. You may have been at the receiving end of this behaviour or realise you've behaved this way too. It's uncomfortable, isn't it? This is a step away from feeling centred, authentic and being true to yourself. It's a sign of nervous system dysregulation. Now, imagine feeling safe to admit your vulnerabilities and your errors. Imagine being met with emotionally mature communication, instead of the other person retaliating and lashing out.

Projection is when someone unconsciously attributes their thoughts and feelings on to someone else.

definition

Feeling safe in a relationship, whether with a partner, friend or family member, is the crux for honest communication. If you don't feel safe, or confident in yourself, you may resort to defensive behaviours to protect yourself from being vulnerable, which can be an incredibly uncomfortable place to be. Defensiveness usually arises from perceived threat, criticism or emotional discomfort, and it can be a coping mechanism to protect someone from low self-esteem, guilt or shame. Holding an awareness of what the defensiveness may be protecting, and not releasing blame or responsibility, can help create space for empathy and compassion. It's not easy but it's refreshing to hear someone say, 'I mucked up. I'm sorry but I want to fix this' or 'I'm having a bad day and really not myself', instead of shutting down or not engaging. Owning what it is to be human in that moment can contribute so much to reconciliation and understanding and creates the opportunity for the other person to be receptive or be able to support you. Defensiveness and projection can close the door to support and effective communication. It can lead to conflict and misunderstanding and prevents opportunity for repair and growth. Owning your behaviour, on the other hand, can inspire others to be more honest too. Beautiful growth happens around witnessing others' growth. It's called mirroring.

Mirroring is an unconscious action where we imitate someone else's behaviours. For example, if someone is talking in a slow, kind and calm manner with us, we will tend to interact back in a slow and calm manner. Positive behaviours, such as honesty, self-care and healthy relationships, can also be mirrored.

definition

Whilst defence mechanisms are behind many behavioural patterns, it's also important to consider how factors such as shame, guilt, anxiety, mental illness, stress, attachment styles and trauma affect someone's behaviour too. For example, being stressed may cause you to feel utterly overwhelmed and not have the energy to reply to someone's text. Having an insecure attachment style (as we explored in Chapter Two) may lead this person to feel jealous and untrusting. Shame may lead someone to hide their true self, making it difficult for them to form deep connections, no matter how hard you try. I am yet to see someone not soften with empathy when this shift of perspective is explored. Seeing someone through the lens through which they see themselves can result in us changing the way we relate to them. I once had a client who wanted to call their partner straight after their session to start reconciling their differences as they were able to consider the possible reasons behind their partner's behaviour. They had become very focused on their partner's inability to communicate their feelings and considered them to be generally emotionally unavailable. When I invited them to share a little more about their partner, it materialised that they had lost their mother when they were three and had grown up with their elderly grandmother and a father who was emotionally unavailable. There were traits of possible avoidant attachment and a deep inner wound of loss, which may have contributed to a fear of sharing vulnerability and abandonment. Inviting my client to hold space for their partner's own story enabled something to shift in themselves, which looked like understanding and empathy. Sometimes we can't see our own wounds and how they may impact our relationships but when others hold space for us, we may find spaces that feel safer to grow within. This is healing.

Whilst we can't change people, we can change how we respond to them. And when we understand their behaviour, it can be transformative. And this happens time and time again in couples therapy, too: when one partner hears the other partner's side of the story, hears them express their feelings or share their vulnerability, a different perspective can be explored and a new understanding can be uncovered. Aren't we all just desperate to be understood?

Despite this, we are not encouraged to share our vulnerability, are we? To wear it on our sleeve or to be honest about how we are feeling, to use transparency over defensiveness. It doesn't feel safe to do so for many. So, ruptures happen. People feel frustrated, angry, lost or confused as they navigate someone else's 'unreasonable' behaviour. Understanding others does not excuse someone's behaviour but rather is an important tool in how you choose to respond.

Our response truly has the power to change the trajectory of every conversation. When we offer understanding over judgement, we create space for something healthier in the relationship to evolve.

The importance of compassion and understanding others

In an ideal world we can see how meeting someone with compassion and understanding over judgement could be a wonderful model to withhold. Let's imagine a scenario where someone arrives home from work, stressed and agitated, and they end up responding in a short and irritable manner to their partner. In turn, the partner, who has also had a stressful day, may react defensively, leading to escalating tension and possible conflict. These reactions might involve projecting their own frustrations on to each other, further complicating the situation.

Now, let's consider the alternative: the partner at home recognises the unsaid stress, and responds with compassion and reassurance. The tension dissipates. Or maybe the partner coming home from work communicates that they are stressed and need a moment to decompress. How we respond to one another truly matters in these moments.

These responses both require emotional maturity and capacity. And this can be difficult when both partners are dealing with their own challenging circumstances and stress. In a more effective, alternative approach, both partners can take ownership of their stress, openly communicate about their tough days and understand each other's needs instead of projecting their feelings on to one another. Can you see how this approach fosters a more supportive connection?

Ultimately, couples should acknowledge that they are on the same side.

Capacity refers to someone's ability to cope with their emotions, stress levels, mental processes and levels of empathy. Lack of self-care or support, poor health, stress, mental health and someone's personal circumstances all contribute to reduction in capacity.

definition

Imagine you're running late to work and nothing is going to plan on your journey, even the queue at your favourite coffee shop is too long and you don't have time to wait for your usual takeaway. When you arrive at work, you feel frazzled and stressed. You may snap at your colleague, but instead of them snapping back or passing judgement, they ask if you're OK. They ask if you need anything, or even better, they offer to grab you a coffee. Can you feel your nervous system start to calm in this scenario? Your shoulders drop, your breath becomes a little deeper and your heart rate slows. Your nervous system may have stayed dysregulated for longer, making focusing on work so much harder, if your colleague hadn't been so kind. Coming back to feeling safe to show our humanness can also change the trajectory of a situation.

Let's say you're on the train and someone barges past you, knocks your phone on the floor and glances back, but doesn't apologise. You reach to pick it up, as they put their head down and storm past. It's easy to feel riled by this display of rudeness, but imagine asking, 'What happened to them to make them behave this way?' Maybe they're unhappy at home. Maybe they had their own bad morning. They're exhibiting defensive behaviour, not acknowledging blame. Maybe they have a lack of self-confidence or low self-worth. Shifting your mindset to this way of thinking can change your reaction. It doesn't excuse their behaviour, but it can help diffuse it. Having compassion and understanding enables you to help keep your own nervous system from becoming dysregulated by feelings of irritation and frustration.

But compassion can be hard in practice, not because we are uncaring but because it requires us to come from a place of calm and regulation ourselves. Our own difficulties can make this challenging. It can also be difficult to witness someone else's behaviour and know how to respond helpfully, especially when witnessing someone's pain or sadness. We may feel uncomfortable and not know how to be supportive. But imagine if you were going through something painful, and a friend sat with you through that pain and offered you love and support. Imagine you were really stressed about an upcoming event, and someone offered you love and care. Someone saw the unsaid.

Being able to offer compassion comes from having capacity within yourself. It comes from noticing when you are struggling and building resilience and capacity to help others. It is about acknowledging the work you may need to do to be able to meet people where they are at. Being the person you need in that moment can be a beautiful place to start.

Give a sunflower sun and watch it bloom. Compassion over judgement changes everything. Hurt people move differently in the face of compassion.

Resilience refers to someone's ability to bounce back during tough times. Not in a toxic positivity way, but in the ability to meet their needs when faced with hard times, manage their emotions, reach out when needed and be able to move forward. I often think that resilience is a harsh word and impies that we have to be strong, so whilst I understand it's great to be able to find ways to best handle things, I prefer to think of it as our personal resources we have access to for caring for ourselves on the good and bad days. Resilience can be built through practising self-care, building and maintaining support systems around you, as well as seeking help when needed and learning from past experiences of what worked and what didn't work.

definition

On compassion

Compassion is an emotional state we feel within that holds deep love, care and awareness of the suffering of others with a want to help free them from it. When experiencing compassion, you may find yourself offering empathy, kindness and understanding as a means to help. And, although empathy and compassion are often used in place of one another, there is a subtle difference. Empathy is defined as having the ability to understand and share the feelings of another, as if you were experiencing the hurt yourself. Compassion shares many of empathy's components, but with the added emotional reaction for the person's wellbeing and a want to actively help. Empathy can manifest as, 'Oh, that sounds awful, I really feel for you', compared to compassion, 'Oh, that sounds awful, and I really feel for you, what can I do to help?'

The benefits of compassion are vast. It enables you to connect with others at a much deeper level and helps build healthier relationships. Someone being shown compassion may experience reduced symptoms of depression and anxiety, reduced stress levels and reduced feelings of aloneness. These all have a direct influence on the regulation of the nervous system. It can make you feel calmer, which can reduce your heart rate and reduce feelings of tension. Receiving compassion helps promote a healthier state within the body's internal systems, which leads to boosting overall mental wellbeing and longevity. And the benefits are not just for the person suffering: the pleasure centres in the brain when we experience joy from eating chocolate or socialising with friends are equally as active as when we offer someone compassion.

How different emotions manifest in behaviour

- **Shame:** a complex emotion where the person views that something is deeply wrong with them. This may manifest in behaviours such as withdrawing, experiencing low self-worth and feeling unlovable.

- **Guilt:** an emotion whereby the person feels that they have done something deeply wrong; it can lead to avoiding people and self-sabotaging behaviours such as self-harm, substance misuse and any other form that feels like self-punishment.

- **Addiction:** can be a result of early life experiences contributing to complex trauma, or PTSD, anything to numb the pain. But this can also be a result of mental illness, poor mental health and social problems. Again, the question of what happened can be so important over judgement. Addiction is fundamentally someone's attempt to self-soothe.

- **Projection:** a psychological defence mechanism whereby a person unconsciously attributes their deemed negative feelings, thoughts and behaviours on to others in terms of blame, denial and anger. Projection comes from poor self-worth, low self-confidence and may be hiding shame or guilt.

- **Insecure attachment:** the way we behave as adults in relationships can be deeply rooted in early life experiences with our primary caregiver/caregivers. Of course, other factors may play a role such as trauma, previous relationship history and genetics. And with only just over 50 per cent of adults being thought to be securely attached, there's a large proportion who are experiencing feelings of insecure attachment. This may manifest as a person being anxious, craving closeness and fearing abandonment, so they may be clingy. Or it may manifest as a person being avoidant and they may avoid getting too close to someone and be fiercely independent (as covered in Chapter Two).

- **Anger:** a normal emotion but it is often hiding an unmet need within the person (see page 24 in Chapter One).

- **Passive aggression:** an emotion where anger or frustration are expressed subtly, such as through insincere compliments, silent treatment, gossip, mean jokes, doing a task intentionally poorly or sarcasm. The behaviours may be an attempt to mask difficulties in expressing a person's emotions, insecurity, a fear of direct confrontation or a lack of confidence.

This is a simple overview of some behaviours, and the nuances and complexities of these states are vast, but they can be helpful to hold an awareness of, when coming from a place of understanding over judgement. Most often, the manifesting behaviours are not personal to you, although they really can feel like it at the time. Working on your own self-worth and sense of self can be important here to safeguard you from taking things personally, which may result in your own inner peace and mental wellbeing being challenged. This is an example of leaning into an awareness of your own truth.

Ways to show compassion when someone is struggling

When someone you love is struggling, it can be so painful to witness, and your first response might be to jump in and try to fix it and offer a solution to help them feel better. But taking a moment to appreciate that you may not know what they need in that moment is a key step. So often our response is based on what we ourselves consider that we may need in that moment and, as our lives and the lens we see the world through are not the same, how can we possibly know? The same dilemma surfaces in the therapy room. For many, it can be incredibly painful to sit with someone in their discomfort but being able to be alongside someone in their pain can be so healing for people. And as tempting as it is for me to want to offer solutions, just being there and holding space for my clients is where the healing process can evolve.

Ways to offer compassion that may open space for healing can look like:

- 'I'm here.'

- 'That sounds really hard.'

- 'What do you need right now?'

- 'I hear you.'

- 'Is there anything I can do to help?'

- 'It's understandable you feel that way.'

- 'I really care about you.'

- 'Your words are safe with me.'

- 'I'm not here to judge.'

- 'It's OK not to feel OK right now.'

- 'You're not alone in this, I'm here.'

These phrases allow the person on the receiving end to feel validated, heard and supported. It also helps them maintain their autonomy in the moment. Next time you feel tempted to step in and offer advice, maybe take a step back and just be there for them.

Being heard and seen is a beautiful example of compassion and can be beautifully healing.

Six ways to cultivate more compassionate behaviours

1. **Practise self-compassion:** Be kind to yourself, notice the thoughts you're having without judgement. Notice the way your body reacts to this compassion over judgement. Your body is a wealth of information if you connect with it. Use these felt sensations to warm to sharing compassion with others.

2. **Carry out random acts of kindness:** Offer to help someone, let someone go first, hold the door open, donate to charity. Incorporate these daily acts of kindness whilst being mindful of the ripple effect of this kindness.

3. **Practise mindfulness:** Become more present in your everyday rituals to become more aware of your thoughts and feelings. Having a deeper awareness of our own thoughts and feelings can help cultivate compassion for how others may be feeling (think sonder).

4. **Volunteer in your community:** This brings feelings of worth as well as enabling you to connect within your community through compassion. More exposure to helping meet other people's needs increases the pleasure responses in the brain (think dopamine).

5. **Listen:** Listen to not respond and share your own story, but to make the other person feel truly heard without interruption. Consider how you feel when someone offers you this beautiful way of communicating.

6. **Practise empathising:** Take the time to consider how you would feel in someone else's shoes. Pay attention to the sensations you may feel in your body, such as observing whether there is heaviness or sadness. Practising empathy this way can help shift the way we may respond to someone.

Journal prompts for cultivating more compassion

- What are ways that you could show yourself compassion?

- How does that make you feel as opposed to when you meet yourself with judgement?

- If you're unable to show yourself compassion, can you name the feelings that arise? What self-talk or beliefs are holding you back? What may the cause of these beliefs be?

- What is one small way that you can reframe those negative thoughts? Think about what you'd say to a friend.

- Reflect on a time that someone has shown you compassion. Describe how you felt. What is a way you can cultivate those feelings to share with others?

- Think of a situation with someone where you may struggle to understand their behaviour and reflect on how you can think of them differently. What are the reasons you struggle? Can you find empathy in what you do know of their life? Are there aspects of their life that you have little information on? Would a more empathic and understanding approach change the way you may meet them?

- If you find being compassionate difficult in terms of capacity, what self-care do you need to give yourself to create more room for others?

- What is one small thing you can do each day to cultivate a more compassionate approach in your life?

Offering compassion is a beautiful gift for someone who is struggling. Just taking a moment to hold an awareness of how it would feel to be judged, of how it would feel to be isolated and alone, of how it would feel to be so totally misunderstood, and then imagining someone meeting you with understanding and compassion. Is there anything kinder in that moment when you may be feeling so lost?

On Healing

Chapter Seven

You deserve to heal so that you can:

- feel safe.

- develop a deeply secure attachment to self.

- understand that your needs matter.

- trust yourself.

- befriend your nervous system.

- validate yourself.

- forgive yourself.

- understand yourself.

- start to like yourself again.

- be there for yourself.

What is healing?

> **Emotional wounds** refer to a lasting emotional injury that occurs as a result of an upsetting or traumatic event. These wounds can result from (and this is not an exhaustive list) betrayal by a close friend or family member, from rejection, grief, end of a relationship, abuse, humiliation, abandonment, failure and trauma, causing feelings of hurt, shame, guilt, anger or sadness. These wounds can affect a person's sense of self, ability to trust and their overall mental wellbeing.
>
> *definition*

The Ancient Greeks used the word 'therapeuo' for healing. And although it was primarily used for healing physical health, it also recognised the emotional and spiritual wellbeing elements of healing we recognise today. We now think of emotional healing as the way to heal from emotional wounds or traumas that we experienced in the past and still cause us pain. We sometimes shy away from the word 'heal', as it has connotations of being broken, as if something is deeply wrong at our core that we may feel shame to admit even to ourselves. Yet we aren't broken. Sometimes we just need compassionate help in guiding ourselves home to a place that feels safer. And to me, the Greek word 'therapeuo', from where our word therapy originates, offers comfort to the word 'heal'. It feels less isolating, less inferring of brokenness and more embodying of a process of togetherness.

As a therapist, I see healing at its rawest. I see emotional wounds, the hurt held within, where there simply aren't words to describe the enormity of its vastness of immense feeling. Souls hiding, feelings suppressed, bodies a cavern of painfully held memories, preventing fulfilled happy living. Stories draped in swathes of darkness when even the smallest glimmers of light, such as compassion, safety, courage or hope, could bring some release, some ease, some lessening of the pain.

I'm reminded of the Japanese art, Kintsugi, where broken pottery is put back together with gold, providing a beautiful metaphor for embracing your flaws and imperfections. It gives light to the parts that we once considered broken and shows their beauty. It symbolises the art of self-forgiveness as we learn to accept the cracks and see them as imperative to our beauty. And maybe that's what is at the core of healing, a forgiveness to self for hiding the pain, for believing we were at fault, for choosing for so long to not meet ourselves with self-compassion.

Healing is complex. Humans are complex. And emotional wounding is complex. Maybe it looks like healing from trauma, from relational trauma, from generational trauma (we'll cover this more later in the chapter). Everyone's experience comes from a different place so everyone's healing will look different too. Yet, the very essence of healing remains the same for all: it is a journey, moving from a place of emotional pain and trauma to a place of wellbeing, resilience and inner peace, where the wounds of the past have less of a hold and life feels a little freer. It's a journey where capacity for more ease has a chance of being created.

Healing is growth. And this growth can take many different forms. There's an awareness needed, a compassionate responsibility to self as well as honesty that our current patterns of behaviour aren't helping us flourish. Maybe you repeat unhealthy patterns in relationships, maybe you continuously berate yourself for not being enough, maybe you don't trust yourself and get frustrated that you can't make decisions for your own life with confidence, maybe you struggle to put your needs first, maybe you struggle to even know what your needs are, maybe you don't consider yourself to matter. When we allow ourselves the gift of healing, we can begin to understand ourselves at a deeper level, understand where our patterns of behaviour may have come from and learn that, in so many cases, our behaviours are a result of coping mechanisms learned in childhood.

And I hope, within each of the chapters of this book, that you find words to encourage you on your healing journey, to open space for you to grow because it is through the process of understanding yourself that healing and growth can happen. With insight, awareness and, ultimately, choosing you, healing can have a chance. Some steps to starting your healing journey are covered later in this chapter.

Our behaviours and coping mechanisms can often be referred to as creative adjustments. They are the ways we create to adjust to our environment. You may use humour to hide pain because you've learned that people respond more positively to humour than sitting with you in your pain. You may overtalk because it feels unbearable to sit in silence. You may become overly self-sufficient because you learned that help wasn't there in the past when you needed it. You may make yourself very small because to take up space wasn't safe. You may put other people's needs first because you weren't taught that your needs matter too. You may carry these creative adjustments with you through life, rarely taking the time to question how they help you. Yes, they may have been necessary in the past to help you cope best, but are they helping you now in adulthood? Probably not, but unless you bring the behaviours to light, be honest with yourself, you may continue to use them and they may become part of your personality.

We are wired for survival. We don't stop and consider whether something is good for us. If it helps us survive and get through, then our body adapts to keep surviving. And until we learn that maybe our experience that created the need for creative adjustments wasn't healthy, they take their toll on us. Escapism can manifest through endless scrolling on social media, procrastination, substance misuse or continually avoiding our feelings. These things may affect the way we interact with others if we struggle to be present and authentic. So, our relationships are affected, our sense of self is affected, our ability to meet our own needs is affected as we ignore our unhealthy patterns of behaviour. These core ways of behaving have more of an impact on our life than we consciously realise, but offering ourselves the awareness to look at what the behaviours may be masking, although not without acknowledging the bravery it takes, can benefit our mental wellbeing hugely as we create space for understanding the reason for endless scrolling and what we are avoiding or trying to escape from. Perhaps, healing can help you start to address the life challenges you are struggling with and escaping from. Think of the benefits of healing and growth where there's contentment over continued stress, a sense of freedom over feeling stuck, an ability to communicate over allowing feelings to be bottled up inside causing emotional turmoil, improved relationships over constant indecipherable angst, validating ourselves over needing someone else's approval. This is healing. This is growth.

Self-understanding and self-awareness enable us to start the process of healing the parts that have required us to hold on to those creative adjustments to avoid the challenges that are underneath the behaviour. We can't heal if we don't have the awareness. And whilst, for some, profound growth can come from continued self-work, such as meditation, mindfulness, movement, rest, connection and journalling practices, others may require a deeper level of work with the support of professionals if continued self-work isn't lessening the impact of the manifestations of the core wounds impacting their day-to-day life. Our healing helps us to find a way to be seen, to be heard and to feel we can live as our authentic selves both for ourselves and for the relationship we have with others, without carrying the heaviness of the unhealed work.

Identifying those unhealthy patterns

Healing requires inward listening. Yet this can be so challenging for some. The nuances of healing and growth are vast in terms of experienced trauma and lived experiences in general. But there's a fundamental need in healing to bring the mind and body into alignment so that an awareness of your thoughts, how they affect your emotions and the way your nervous system answers, guides how you live your life.

Notice whether you feel at ease or whether you're living a life that makes sense, one that feels safe and one that's aligned. It's an invitation to self-reflect with honesty but with a dose of self-belief that going a little deeper, peeling back those layers to understanding, will, in fact, help you longer term. It's an invitation to write a new story going forward, to enable you to be the author instead of someone else's past behaviour having a hold and writing your story for you. It's a journey of finding self-trust through connecting with gentle curiosity to the way your body responds.

Your story may not have been started by you but how it unfolds can be up to you.

And that requires bringing to awareness what is no longer helping you flourish. It requires gentle and compassionate self-responsibility to knowing that the next step can be up to you.

We all have unhealthy patterns of behaviour from time to time, such as overspending, too much screentime or having one too many drinks. That's being human. But if these patterns become more consistent and are having a regular negative effect on your day-to-day life, then it may be worth exploring a little more. These unhealthy patterns may be masking hidden messages. For example, maybe you find you're taking regular sick days from work. Maybe you're unhappy at work and not getting enough support or there are issues at home that are making you feel stressed, and you can't cope with work. Or you find you're pouring a glass of wine every night and it regularly turns into a bottle, but it numbs the pain of feeling, and it doesn't feel safe to feel right now. Or maybe you've become obsessed with exercise and can't allow yourself to take a day off because those unkind taunts from other children when you were younger have you believing that you're overweight and you never want to go back to hearing that or experiencing that feeling of hurt or shame that you felt then.

And, as hard as it is to do, because it brings the behaviour into your reality, the first step of acknowledging the behaviour is key. From here, you can gently explore what you feel the triggers are. This can be through self-reflection, journalling or speaking to someone you trust. When do you engage in the behaviour? Maybe keep a diary to track any patterns. This is not a practice of blame. It's one of offering mindfulness and self-compassion. It's one of self-love as you move towards knowing that you ultimately don't want the pattern to continue. Imagine what you would say to a friend in this situation. That supportive self-talk can be incredibly helpful. It's compassion in action. And compassion helps the hold of harsh self-judgement lose its grip.

Identifying and doing the work to break unhealthy patterns is challenging but can be helped if you bring to awareness that the patterns come from a deep-rooted place of survival, to numb the pain of feeling, to better cope with your environment. Holding this can help remove the stigma of self-blame and any attached shame, which is so often felt with unhealthy behaviours, and can ease us gently along the journey of forgiveness.

Shame is a deep feeling within that there is something fundamentally wrong with us, almost indescribable, which is why it's hard to talk about, but it loses its fire and its grip when it's given words out loud in safe spaces. As Brené Brown once said, 'Shame, everyone has it. No one wants to talk about it. But the less we talk about it, the more we have of it.' Shame, shared in safe, compassionate spaces, loses the fight. Compassion truly is the antidote to shame.

definition

As was discussed in Chapter Six, there's always a reason for someone's behaviour, so maybe extending the same compassionate question to yourself 'What happened to me to make me behave this way?' would be a kinder place to start.

Notice the tiny shifts that may happen within when you ask yourself that question. Notice how your nervous system responds. This is a process that takes practice, and those tiny shifts can start to increase the more you offer yourself this compassion. It's this compassion that will help create the change. It's this connecting to how the body feels, noticing the release, however tiny, and trusting that it will grow. That healing and growth are possible. Those habits were built on years of adaptation, so finding a way to let go of the expectation that it should happen quickly or be a linear progression to undo is crucial. Think trust and consistency. And know that you don't have to do this journey alone.

Gentle steps to help you heal

Step 1: Recognising the need to heal is key to making a change, to letting go, to being able to trust yourself again and to being able to live a life that enables you to feel safer, freer and more at ease. Ask yourself questions, such as 'What caused a reaction in me today?' or 'Why do I never have luck in relationships?' or 'Do I feel generally happy in my life?' These reflective questions may prompt further exploration to understand and heal.

Step 2: Use self-reflection and self-awareness by exploring the underlying causes of the feelings and the behaviours. Take a moment to just be with yourself to enable yourself to quieten down the outside noise and tap into what is causing your unhappiness, frustration, discontentment. Welcome the thoughts in with compassion and without judgement. There's no right or wrong answer other than just what is presented to you in that moment. Journalling and time in nature can help this process of self-reflection.

Step 3: Acknowledge the emotions that may come in. How can you process these in a healthy way? What are they trying to tell you? Maybe you're frustrated that you keep spending time with people who make you feel low. Maybe you're feeling overwhelmed with how little time you have for yourself, yet you don't know how to create space. Maybe you feel lonely and don't know how to reach out. Maybe you feel guilt that you can't let go of a mistake. Maybe you feel unhappy with your life but don't know how to make changes. Acknowledging the emotions that are attached to the unhealthy cycle that you're in can help guide the action that may be needed (as was outlined in Chapter One). Allowing yourself to feel and to express is key in identifying the root of the discontentment. Tools such as journalling, meditation or opening up to someone you trust are good ways to explore the emotions a little deeper.

Step 4: Equip yourself with knowledge around healing. This can be obtained through podcasts, blogs, books or online support groups. If something doesn't seem relevant, move on. But if it does, then explore a little deeper in this area. Not everything out there will be applicable to your own personal experience. Deciphering what is and isn't is important here.

Step 5: Challenge any negative thoughts that come in. Can you find ways to reframe them? Are they true? Offer yourself compassion. Is there a pattern to these thoughts? Hold an awareness that having negative thoughts is a normal human experience but come back to rational thought processes and reflect that holding on to negative thoughts can greatly affect your emotions, behaviours and wellbeing. Asking ourselves why we would choose to let the thought have that much power over us can be a helpful tool in the moment.

Step 6: Look towards self-forgiveness and letting go. Holding on to anger, resentment, blame or guilt can affect the healing process by leaving us stuck in the past. Explore ways to speak to yourself as you would to a friend. I talk more about letting go in Chapter Nine. Again, finding ways to healthily process these emotions and coming back to a place where your nervous system can regulate is the answer. When engaged in regulation, we can come back to a place where we feel safer and can view things from a different perspective. Sometimes it can be helpful to see our own role in the situation. Where can we take self-responsibility to move forward?

Step 7: Seek support. One of the most important steps in healing. This can be professional help or help from someone you trust. The co-regulation that ensues from connecting with your safe people lies at the heart of healthy relationships and healing. It facilitates the nourishment and regulation between two nervous systems. It is imperative for our survival.

Step 8: Notice and review. Notice how you feel as you work through these steps. Where is the resistance? What are the sensations you notice in your body? What shifts do you feel within? What happens to your mood? This noticing will help you develop a deeper sense of self-awareness and help in your healing journey. How can you keep building on the shifts within that bring ease? What are the things that bring you back to your connection with self, as we explored in Chapter Five?

A gentle note for you: I hope you find the courage to choose yourself and take the steps to heal and grow. It can be challenging, turning your life upside down, affecting relationships (though the right ones flourish) and making you feel lonely at times. But moving forward can bring clarity, hope and a new way of living that resonates and aligns. There's a deep truth of self that I hope you one day get to see. And whilst on this journey, meet yourself with care. Prioritise rest, sleep, nourishing foods, safe connections and movement to help build strong foundations for healing. You are worth the effort and the path to healing can hold beautiful discoveries of self.

Understanding trauma

Trauma is a lasting emotional response to an intensely stressful and shocking event that impacts our mental and physical wellbeing and can overwhelm a person's ability to cope and can include, though is not limited to:

- **Single event trauma:** such as an accident, sexual abuse, grief, loss or a natural disaster.

- **Complex trauma:** where trauma happens repeatedly over time causing an impact on the development and wellbeing of a person. This is often associated with childhood trauma.

- **Generational trauma:** where one generation, or person in a generation, experiences a single event trauma or complex trauma, and the impact of those traumatic experiences, if not healed, is passed down to future generations by behaviours such as stress or anxiety, which affect the way the next generation is raised. For example, if a caregiver was never taught that their needs matter, if they grew up in a household where one of their own caregivers was not emotionally available or present, they may not know how to meet their own needs as an adult and, therefore, struggle to identify the needs of their child or have the capacity to meet the child's needs. Dysfunctional patterns in generations have a way of being repeated until someone decides to break the cycle.

Mental health manifestation of unhealed trauma may look like addiction, anxiety, depression, low self-worth, people-pleasing behaviours, inability to identify needs, inability to deal with stress, fatigue, disassociation, flashbacks, emotional outbursts, nightmares, fear, emotional suppression, shame and guilt. And unhealed trauma can also take its toll on the body causing physical symptoms, such as accelerated heart rate, headaches, stomach problems, muscle tension, and can lead to the development of chronic illnesses.

If you or someone you know is struggling with unhealed trauma, please know that help is available, and professionals trained in trauma healing can help trauma survivors to live a life that feels safer and bring them back to a deeper regulated connection with themselves. As Dr Peter Levine says, 'The goal of healing is not the eradication of all symptoms but the creation of an empowered and connected life.' Someone struggling with trauma deserves this way of living. And if this resonates for you, I sincerely hope that you find a way to heal from something that was not your fault.

The wider effects of healing

A beautiful aspect to the emotional healing process is the ripple effects that radiate out into the rest of someone's world. Seeing someone heal from the things that should never have happened to them and seeing the way that beauty can have a chance to unfurl within them as they come to understand themselves, are able to regulate, can catch themselves before falling back into old unhealthy patterns of behaviour and, fundamentally, not live in survival mode is wonderfully inspiring and profound.

When we heal, we have fewer unmet needs as healing helps us:

- to identify our needs (through the process of self-awareness)

- to learn to meet them (through self-understanding and self-responsibility)

- to communicate them in a healthy way (through learning to use our voice and building on self-worth).

The process of self-awareness in healing helps there to be a recognition of unhealthy behaviours and a desire to heal from them going forward as we learn that healing brings regulation and we learn that we want to keep feeling that. Unhealed emotional wounds can have a huge impact on someone's capacity to cope. Healing enables people to understand themselves, to learn how to use emotional regulation tools to help them handle life better and live less in emotional nervous system dysregulation. This has a direct impact on their own mental health as well as the health of the relationships around them. Conflict can also be reduced as self-understanding enables us to understand others at a deeper level. If we understand ourselves more, it opens space for us to extend that understanding to others.

Take someone who lashes out at their partner when they feel vulnerable, for example. They may do this instead of coming from a place of healing where they are able to acknowledge the fact that they feel this way. Through healing, they have a stronger sense of self and self-worth. They are able to communicate with their partner, be it, 'I just need some space to calm down, can you give me a moment?' or 'I'm feeling really overwhelmed right now, so can we talk about this later?' Imagine the after effects of this approach compared to lashing out in frustration or defensive projection, such as 'You never give me space' or 'I'm fed up with you going on and on about this, leave me alone.'

Healing can help bring feelings of ease that can ripple through relationships, the impact of which can affect the relationships more than we consciously realise. Healing brings emotional wellbeing. Healing brings authentic connection. Healing brings self-trust. Healing brings self-worth. Healing brings growth. Healing brings finding safer spaces. Healing brings healed future generations as people learn to meet themselves with compassion, emotionally regulate and meet their needs, so that they can meet the needs of the future generations. Healed souls help others without the negative impacts of stress, emotional dysregulation and unhealed emotional wounds that can get in the way of them being present and engaged in a regulated way.

Somatic healing practices for you

1. **Spinal twist:** This can be done either from a sitting or standing position. Twist your spine and look over one shoulder, taking in your environment for a few moments, and then twisting back, look over the other shoulder. Now repeat. This helps orient and ground us.

2. **Self-regulate:** Create a safe self-container. Place your left hand under your right armpit and your right hand on your left arm. Hold for a few moments and if it feels safe to do so, gently rub your hands up and down your skin or gently pat.

3. **Body scan:** This is an active meditation, which brings your focus to the top of your head all the way down to your feet and acknowledges how each body part feels as you scan down slowly and back up. Where you feel tension, breathe a little more deeply and exhale to release the tension until you feel the body part start to relax. If it feels comfortable to do so, tense each muscle group and relax as you move through the body in deep connected awareness.

Journal prompts for healing and growth

- What are some unhealthy behaviours or habits that may not be serving you well for either your physical or emotional wellbeing?

- How do they make you feel long term?

- What are some ways that you can move towards letting go of these habits or behaviours?

- How can you create space for more healthy behaviours?

- Are you able to identify some triggers that may prompt the unhealthy behaviour?

- What are the ways that you can create some space from these triggers?

- What are the underlying beliefs you may have about yourself that are contributing to the unhealthy behaviours?

- Where have these beliefs come from? How can you challenge these thoughts?

- What are some ways that you can incorporate some self-care into your daily routine?

- Who are the people in your life that you could reach out to for help?

I hope you get to fall in love with the process of deep healing, so that you can meet a version of yourself who feels safe, who knows healthy love, who gets to live a life that knows what joy, contentment and peace really feels like.

Chapter Eight

On Energy

A gentle reminder of energy sources:

- Sunlight.

- Movement.

- Laughter.

- Gratitude.

- Meditation.

- Nature.

- Self-care.

- Hydration.

- Journalling.

- Nourishing food.

- Creativity.

- Boundaries.

- Sleep.

- Connection.

Becoming aware of what energises and drains you

I like to think of energy as this delicious resource that is essential to my wellbeing. I can tap into it when needed, and it is imperative that I take an active role in replenishing its levels as a matter of deep self-care, so that I can cope better with my everyday life. Noticing how I feel in relation to how much energy I have and who has access to my energy is an integral part of my ability to function optimally.

Just as important as being aware of my energy resources is that I'm aware of energy drainers. Energy drainers can be workload, disagreements with loved ones, poor sleep, too much screen-time, comparison, perfectionism, other people's negativity, lack of boundaries or anything that activates your nervous system and sends it into its protective state of fight/flight/freeze/fawn. These offer a stark contrast to energy sources, such as creativity, spending time with people who inspire and lift you, long nourishing walks in nature, doing the things that spark joy or simply just taking five minutes for yourself. All of these can help bring you out of the fight/flight/freeze/fawn response and back to a safe connection with self. Remember, having an awareness of how our nervous system moves between these protective states (fight/flight/freeze/fawn) and back to connection can help us learn how energy drainers can have an impact on our body. And this awareness can help guide us towards filling our life with more of the energy givers. Energy givers are the activities that boost our feel-good hormones, such as oxytocin, dopamine, serotonin and endorphins – chemicals in the brain that help regulate our mood and emotions.

Unlock your daily D.O.S.E of feel-good hormones

- **Dopamine (pleasure chemicals):** sleep, personal wins, self-care, listening to music, meditation, sunlight exposure, connection, well-balanced diet to support brain health, hobbies, creativity.

- **Oxytocin (the love hormone):** physical touch, such as holding hands or hugs, self-soothing touch, positive connections with friends and family, laughter, kindness, positive memory creation and recollection, mindfulness, deep breathing.

- **Serotonin (the happy hormone):** sunlight, gratitude, exercise, massage, yoga, reducing stress, self-care, a balanced diet, emotion regulation.

- **Endorphins (pain and stress relievers):** moderate to intense exercise, such as running or dancing, laughter (try watching a funny movie or spending time with funny people), listening to music, meditation, positive connections.

When the balance in our life is leaning towards energy drainers, we can become more and more depleted of the feel-good hormones. This impacts our stress levels and affects our ability to cope, and regulate our mood and our emotions.

Consider how you feel after a nourishing weekend filled with personal time, quality moments with loved ones, a break from work, and activities you enjoy. It's likely that you feel more content once Monday comes. On the other hand, compare this to a hectic weekend with little sleep, work deadlines and the cycle starting all over again on Monday.

The choices we make can either energise or drain us. Repeatedly choosing the 'draining' choices can lead to chronic stress, anxiety, irritability and exhaustion, impacting your long-term mental health and wellbeing. Life is challenging, and it's not always easy to make positive changes. This is not a self-help book that ignores the complexities of life. By becoming more self-aware about how we cope with life's stress and identifying small, manageable steps that bring ease rather than stress, you can gradually make beneficial choices for yourself. It's about recognising these moments of relief and ease and repeating them to create a positive shift.

Consider the water glass analogy as a reflection of our energy capacity. Picture a glass brimming with water – it's so full that even a tiny drop could cause it to overflow. These drops represent your energy drainers, such as lack of sleep, stress, negative influences, strained relationships and concerns about your health. As these drops accumulate, your capacity diminishes, leaving you with less resilience to cope with life's challenges. However, there's a way to increase your capacity. You can consciously lower the water level in the glass by doing things that replenish your energy – your 'energy sources'. This might be soul-nourishing practices, such as yoga, breathwork, journalling or spending time with people who lift you. By embracing these energy-giving practices, you can gradually expand your capacity (lower the water level in the glass). And when inevitable energy drainers enter your life, you have space to navigate them more effectively. The drops won't cause the glass to overflow. I revisit this time and time again when my own glass water level feels too high, and I'd love for you to do the same.

To effectively manage your energy, you need to be intentional about it. Bringing awareness to our energy levels and how our experiences impact us is crucial. Regular check-ins can help with this. You can incorporate them into your existing routines, like during your commute or when brushing your teeth. Take a

moment during these times to reflect on how you felt throughout the day. Were you content, agitated or distracted? Consider
your interactions with others too. Did you enjoy your time with
them or did you feel stressed? Notice any sensations in your body
as you recall these experiences. Being curious here can be transformative as it's what's revealed in this curiosity that will help
you make changes needed. Your goal is to be more mindful of
your energy and to be able to take proactive steps to preserve it.

How to become more mindful and intentional with your energy

Boundaries: they are imaginary lines that create safe spaces,
whether between you and others or different aspects of your life.
They play a crucial role in both your relationships with others
and your relationship with yourself. When used effectively, they
can even strengthen relationships.

It can be helpful to think of metaphors for boundaries, such as
a home with a picket fence, a wall or no boundary around the
home at all. Walls don't let anyone in, good or bad, and can
prevent you from having healthy connections with others. This
can leave you feeling isolated, lonely and disconnected from the
world. Walled boundaries may manifest as inflexible behaviours,
emotional distance as people may tend to keep their feelings to
themselves, avoidance of intimacy and connection, controlling
behaviours and difficulty accepting help. It's helpful to be aware
that these walled boundaries are often put in place as a protective
mechanism deemed necessary as a result of past hurt or trauma.
Picket fences, with a gate, enable you to feel connected to the
world – you can see over the top of them, but you can also open
the gate to let people in and keep others out. You are the owner
of the gate and can choose when you feel safe to open it, for

how long and who is able to come through it. This is your gate, your choice and your personal power. Those using the picket fence analogy to boundaries tend to have a stronger sense of self where they have increased levels of self-awareness, confidence and self-belief. But having no walls at all becomes confusing. This lack of boundaries leaves us exposed, vulnerable and unsafe. Without walls, you may struggle to say no, take on other people's drama, overshare, be easily influenced or have difficulty creating and maintaining space for yourself.

Imagine a draining friendship where you can set a time limit boundary for phone calls or time spent together instead of cutting off the relationship entirely. This allows you to enjoy your friend's company and be supportive all whilst using a boundary, like a picket fence. Whilst cutting someone off entirely creates a walled boundary. If we don't respect our boundaries and we let them become too loose, spending excessive time with the friend, it can lead to frustration and reduced capacity for enjoyable interactions. Healthy boundaries (picket fence) strengthen relationships, whilst loose or walled boundaries compromise them.

But boundaries can be undeniably tricky. You can feel uncomfortable about how the other person may react or what they may think of you. You may embody the other person's feelings and lose sight of the reason you set the boundary in the first place. How someone feels about your boundary is a result of their own self-work. Emotional maturity around boundary setting is paramount for both parties.

Which areas of setting boundaries do you find most tricky? Maybe it's around self-confidence where you feel you don't have the communication skills to set the boundary, or self-worth, where maybe you don't think you matter as much as the other person. Maybe you struggle with people pleasing and saying no. Identifying these areas can be both hugely beneficial and enlightening as a first step to moving forward. Boundary setting can be uncomfortable at first, but when you work on your sense of self (more on this in Chapter Two), boundary setting can become easier. You can feel more connected to yourself, you understand yourself better, feel more confident in your truths and have a higher regard for your self-worth. One of the biggest advantages of setting a boundary is that it can keep you emotionally and physically safe. It can help improve mental health, and boundaries are a key part of healthy relationships. They enable you to show up in relationships in a way that you feel comfortable. And how you set those boundaries shows others how you would like to be treated. Boundaries are key in self-respect. For example, suppose you like time alone in your relationship so instead of avoiding your partner, you communicate openly that you enjoy occasional solitude and it's not about them personally. This communication opens space to prevent feelings of hurt or even conflict arising. Clear communication around needed boundaries allows a relationship to flourish, and your boundary setting can also encourage others to feel safer to verbalise their own boundaries comfortably. It's a beautiful display of emotional maturity and reciprocity at play.

Setting boundaries comes with several benefits, including those within yourself. Honouring your alone time is vital, like limiting social media use, getting enough sleep, staying hydrated and avoiding thinking about work on the weekend. Boundaries with yourself can be useful when considering the energy drainers in your life and maintaining a manageable water level in your glass. Gently bringing about awareness of your boundaries will help with nervous system regulation, helping you move away from the protective states of fight/flight/freeze/fawn and come back to your authentic connection with yourself.

Types of boundaries

PHYSICAL BOUNDARIES

These are your personal space, body, touch and physical interactions, especially regarding how much privacy you need, how close people can get to you before you feel uncomfortable and what kind of touch is OK with you. It also refers to meeting your physical needs, such as rest and nourishment.

Examples:

- 'I can't tonight as I want an early night.'

- 'I don't feel comfortable with you standing so close.'

- 'No.'

- 'I will take the time to cook a delicious meal for myself tonight.'

EMOTIONAL BOUNDARIES

These are your right to have your own thoughts, emotions and feelings, without them being criticised or minimised by others. It also refers to not oversharing personal information. Emotional boundaries are also not feeling responsible for the emotions of others.

Examples:

- 'I don't feel comfortable sharing that information with you.'

- 'I'm feeling overwhelmed right now. Can we come back to this conversation at another time?'

- 'I'm having a hard time right now with some things and would really appreciate it if I could talk to you about it.'

MATERIAL BOUNDARIES

These are personal possessions and finances – your right to spend your own money as you choose and to not loan your possessions or finances if you don't feel happy to.

Examples:

- 'Please don't borrow my clothes without asking.'

- 'I feel uncomfortable with you asking me for money.'

- 'I can't work for you for free.'

TIME BOUNDARIES

These include how you spend your time personally, as well as other people's demands on your time. They involve you setting limits and prevent you over committing yourself and enable you to protect your time and energy.

Examples:

- 'I won't be checking my work emails after 5pm.'

- 'I will prioritise rest this weekend.'

- 'I will limit my time with certain people to protect my energy.'

- 'I will ensure time for the energy givers in my life today.'

INTELLECTUAL BOUNDARIES

These include protecting your thoughts, values and opinions and a respect of other people's views and thoughts, too.

Examples:

- 'I'm not comfortable continuing this conversation if you keep making personal attacks.'

- 'I hear what you are saying but that isn't what I consider to be my truth.'

- 'I would like you to listen without interrupting me as I will listen when you are speaking.'

SOCIAL MEDIA BOUNDARIES

These include establishing a set of guidelines for yourself on how you will interact online and how you will protect your privacy.

Examples:

- 'I will unfollow people on social media who make me feel bad about being me.'

- 'I will block, mute or unfollow anyone who violates my safety.'

- 'I will stop scrolling if I feel lower in mood than when I picked up my phone.'

- 'I will have phone-free days.'

PROFESSIONAL BOUNDARIES

These include appropriate behaviours in the workplace, interactions with others to ensure a healthy, supported work environment, as well as boundaries around appropriate work practices.

Examples:

- 'I don't feel comfortable discussing my private life at work.'

- 'What you're asking me to do isn't in my job description, please could we discuss further?'

- 'I feel I need more support on what you're asking me to do.'

- 'I'm struggling with my mental health, could I take some time off or look to ways to be more supported with this at work?'

How to set boundaries

When setting boundaries, it's normal to worry about how others will respond. You might worry about upsetting people or appearing uncaring or fear the possible conflict that may ensue. Even as I write this, I'm aware of my own 'I'm less important' mindset that often surfaces when thinking about setting my boundaries with others. This sneaky voice stems from feelings of lack of self-worth that so many of us may struggle with. Whilst there's no magic answer to make boundary setting completely easy, recognising its necessity is a crucial first step. Approach the process with curiosity and self-awareness, paying attention to how your body feels when setting boundaries. There's valuable information there if we listen closely. As Rumi said, 'There's a voice that doesn't use words, listen.' Setting one boundary can lead to an easier process for subsequent ones, especially when you experience benefits to your mental health. Like anything, practice and experience make it more manageable. Notice the small shifts you feel inside and build upon them.

Setting boundaries with kindness

Step 1: Allow some reflection time to establish what boundary you need to meet your needs. This will help prevent reactionary boundary setting (unless immediately needed and you feel unsafe) and will enable a considered response to a boundary (focus on taking the heat out of a situation where necessary).

Step 2: Remember the reason you're setting the boundary. Keep your focus on your needs and feelings. You matter, too.

Step 3: Use 'I' statements. This helps remove any attacking or blame. 'I need some space to process my feelings right now.' 'I'm feeling unable to have this conversation right now, can we come back to it another time?' 'I'm not sure if that works for me, can I come back to you?'

Step 4: Timing is key. Choose a time when you're less likely to react over respond. Give yourself the space to come back to connect with yourself. And give yourself the space where you're going to be heard without phones or distractions, and not at the end of a stressful day, for example. Finding the perfect time for these conversations isn't always easy but it can help that you choose a time where you feel you will be heard. Again, this is not applicable if a boundary is needed immediately and you're in danger.

Step 5: Check your tone of voice and posture. Most of the time people hear the way we say something as opposed to the words. Body language and non-verbal communication speak very loudly.

Step 6: Consider the other person's needs, too. Allow space for active listening. Boundary setting is more likely to be effective when understanding, compassion and empathy come into play. The way we set boundaries reflects emotional maturity.

Step 7: Hold an awareness that boundaries are part of self-care. They are a way to look after your mental wellbeing and are not a rejection of others. This awareness can help set the tone of the communication.

Active listening is a style of communication with care. It's a process of fully listening, being present in the conversation, bringing empathy and compassion, and noticing the other person's body language, whilst holding space for them to speak without interruptions and listening to respond instead of listening to say what you want to say with little acknowledgement for the other person's words or feelings.

definition

How people respond to your boundary setting gives you a lot of information about them and the space they are in. For example, how wonderful is it to hear 'No problem' instead of showing signs of discontent with you. Or 'Thank you for letting me know how you feel, let's talk this through and try to repair this situation' instead of body language of resentment or silent treatment. But it's also important to acknowledge that defensive reactions can be due to their own feelings of abandonment, fear of rejection, lack of self-worth, self-importance, defensiveness, issues with control and fear of change. It's rarely personal and inevitably highlights some areas of self-work and reflection for them, too. It can be helpful to keep bringing the focus back to your needs, how a relationship will benefit long term, or how your stress levels will reduce at work, and prevent being taken advantage of or feeling exhausted or not considered. You matter, too.

Boundaries aren't for keeping people out (well, sometimes they are!), they are for keeping the right people in.

When considering the boundaries in your life, it can be helpful to reflect on why they are needed and to be honest with yourself that they aren't a replacement for avoiding challenging situations. True growth blooms from when boundaries are set intentionally from a place of self-awareness, so that they become tools for empowerment rather than avoidance.

Deciding if a boundary is needed

Step 1: Find a quiet comfortable space where you can reflect without interruptions and take a few deep breaths to ground yourself.

Step 2: Reflect on the situation or issue where you feel there might need to be a boundary and notice how your body reacts. What sensations do you feel? Any tension anywhere? What emotions do you feel? Sadness? Frustration? Is there a pattern to the situation? Any warning signs?

Step 3: What boundary could you reasonably set? Would this help the situation?

Step 4: Imagine the boundary being set and notice any sensations your body may have. Relief? Ease? A knowing that it needs to be set?

Step 5: Is the boundary easy to set? If not, what is the resistance?

Step 6: What are the consequences of not setting the boundary? Notice how your body reacts.

Step 7: Is there someone you can ask for support or guidance?

Step 8: What boundary can you set that feels safe and realistic at this moment?

Step 9: Reflect on the boundary and repeat steps 1-7 if the initial boundary has little effect.

Affirmations to empower you when setting a boundary

- My needs matter and deserve to be respected.

- I have the right to protect my time and energy.

- Setting boundaries is an act of self-care and necessary for my mental health.

- I am not responsible for other people's emotional response to my boundary.

- Other people's negative emotional response to my boundary is not a reason not to set one.

- I can set a boundary and still be a kind person.

- It's OK to be me and not who others want me to be.

- It's OK to say no.

- Taking care of my mental health is a priority.

Journal prompts for setting boundaries

- What areas of my life energise me? How can I include more of that energy in my day?

- What areas of my life drain me? What is a boundary I can put in place to reduce this feeling?

- What makes me feel overwhelmed? How can I reduce the overwhelm?

- Which people in my life lift me up? How can I spend more time with them?

- Which people drain me? What boundary is needed here?

- Where can I create space in my life for more joy?

- Where can I create space in my life for rest?

- Who do I feel in my life doesn't honour my boundaries?

- What is a way I can work on that boundary setting?

- What is my previous relationship with setting boundaries? Do I honour them?

- What are my needs? How can I meet them?

- What is one small step today that I can take to make sure I respect my boundaries?

Sometimes we need to remind ourselves that we matter, too. Our needs, our feelings, our thoughts, our joy, our moments, our beautiful lived experiences, our very own lives. Give yourself space to take up even more space in your own beautiful life.

On Letting Go

Chapter Nine

Maybe you find it hard to let go because:

- it really hurts.

- you really cared.

- you thought you would never have to.

- you'd created a story with a different ending.

- it's scary.

- your reality feels unfamiliar without them.

- you don't know this version of you.

- they mattered.

- you felt unfairly treated.

- they brought out a version of you that you miss.

- it was left unfinished.

- you've still got things to say.

- they felt like home.

Why letting go is hard

We can get caught up in stories, can't we? We weave narratives about our relationships, our lives and our futures, imagining how they will unfold. And, as we write these stories, we find comfort and security, settling into feelings of safety with the endings we've created. Yet, the reality doesn't always follow our scripts, does it? A partner may leave, a relationship breaks down or we may face hurt, rejection or changing friendships. But our body felt safe with that previously written story of what we thought would happen even though it was just a story. But they were our stories.

What we must remember, though, is that in our beautifully written stories, we never truly knew the ending. We couldn't predict what was going to happen. And when life does take a different turn, we find ourselves having to adapt almost abruptly to this new reality. And feelings of fear, heartbreak, unfamiliarity and profound loss may arise. Our nervous system craves familiarity as it provides a sense of safety and security. It can feel dysregulated without it. But letting go requires us to feel a new familiarity and how we cope with that can be inextricably linked to our attachment styles, our self-worth and our previous lived experiences with endings. This is why you may see some people move on so easily whilst others struggle for months, even years. Our basic survival instinct is to attach. Humans crave attachment for survival. Our need for others is imperative to our wellbeing, healthy nervous system regulation and ultimate survival. Relationship ruptures can affect at a deeper level because of these survival instincts. But how we cope may also be dependent on our previous attachment experiences (as we explored in Chapter Two).

Let's consider someone with secure attachment (as discussed in Chapter Two). It's not that they won't feel the pain of heartbreak, but they tend to have the advantage of having learned healthy ways to sit with their emotions, understand them, have the tools to healthily regulate and know how to reach out for support. It's this ability to reach out to a support system that can help immensely. And with secure attachment enabling individuals to have a deeper sense of self, there comes an increased self-belief, which can help in processing the breakup and still helping them feel that they matter and are worthy of love going forward. There's emotional capacity to acknowledge the breakup and find a way to move on.

If someone has an avoidant-style attachment (as highlighted in Chapter Two), they may struggle to process their emotions after a breakup or a rupture and tend to suppress their feelings, struggle to learn from the breakup and are less able to self-reflect due to the want to avoid the feeling. This can lead to unhealthy numbing behaviours of the feelings as well as avoidance in taking any responsibility in the breakup/rupture. Someone with an avoidant attachment style may then not see their part in the breakup and may be more likely to feel very bitter and resentful towards their partner. Can you see how it would be more difficult for someone with this attachment style to get closure on a relationship breakdown? It's because their tendencies to suppress would prevent them from processing the breakup fully if they continued to avoid the issue.

If we consider someone with an anxious attachment (previously discussed in Chapter Two), they crave safety, intimacy and closeness and may need constant reassurance from their partner to feel safe and can fear abandonment. This style of attachment can make breakups particularly challenging as they lack self-worth and need others to 'complete' them. Someone with this attachment style craves the feeling of safety again and may make continuous attempts to get back together with their ex. They may struggle more than other attachment styles to let go, to move on and to have belief in themselves on how to process their emotions and work through them as this was not healthily modelled to them as a child.

Can you see how understanding letting go through the lens of attachment helps us understand ourselves a little deeper in how we may respond to letting go of anything that may cause ruptures in our lives? Not necessarily just romantic breakups but even how we respond to friendship issues, work issues, being let down or someone being unkind. How we feel about ourselves and our ability to process can be attributed to those early attachment bonds. However, those attachment bonds aren't fixed or rigid. In fact, we may find ourselves having elements of different attachment styles. Attachment theory is heavily nuanced. It's also helpful to recognise that previous experiences of how we've handled letting go of things can play a part in terms of what went well and what didn't. Identifying any patterns from these experiences can be enlightening for you and help you to become more self-aware.

Take a moment to reflect on whether any of the attachment styles we discussed resonated with you. It's natural to feel curious about what these reflections brought up for you. This introspection can be valuable in understanding yourself better and uncovering areas you might want to explore further. Understanding our reactions to letting go, whilst being aware of why it can be challenging, can be important work as it empowers us to find healthier ways to navigate the process of letting go.

How to let go of things no longer serving you

Letting go is a deeply personal journey, and our individual experiences are complex. Letting go looks different for each one of us and it is neither something that can be rushed nor is it easy to achieve, no matter how much we wish it were that simple. I understand that it's not as easy as flipping an on/off switch whenever we want to. That feeling of knowing something doesn't have the same hold over us like it once did doesn't just happen. It takes time – your time and the work you do in that time. I know how easy it is to get caught up in the idea that we 'should' be over something by now. I've heard this from many of my clients. But something rather wonderful happens when their 'not being able to get over it more quickly' is validated. It's like a weight is lifted and their feelings are understood. Letting go is a process, and it's one that unfolds in its own time, at its own pace, with self-trust, self-value, self-reflection and the work you do that works for you during that time to heal.

Life is a flowing river, shaped by rocks and boulders along its path. As the river encounters these obstacles, it doesn't force its way through; instead, it gracefully adapts, changes direction and keeps flowing around them. Now, imagine the water is frozen. The water cannot flow past the rocks and boulders in its path. It feels stuck and unable to let go. Like frozen water, we're unable to flow when trapped in this state. But just as frozen water needs heat to start flowing again, we need to find our own heat to create flow again. That 'heat' can be a combination of self-love, compassion, gentleness, curiosity, understanding, patience, self-trust and connection. This metaphor helps us to reframe 'getting over' something to the more compassionate thought of 'getting past' or 'flowing past', which can be so healing. Take a moment to think about a challenge you're facing. Imagine adapting, flowing past it, just like the water. Do you notice a shift in how you feel about it? Even the tiniest shift can initiate a change in our nervous system – a step towards healing. Each shift, no matter how small, accumulates over time, fostering a deeper level of self-acceptance. It's a process of allowing these shifts to take root and grow within us, helping us move towards getting past our obstacles. Each shift helps us understand that growth is possible. It helps bring hope to letting go.

Something powerful can happen when we sit with our pain and simply acknowledge that it's hard, that it hurts, without judging ourselves. Offering ourselves this space to feel, without harshly berating ourselves for not being stronger, or that we 'should' be over it, or for being vulnerable can be incredibly nourishing. Taking a step back and asking ourselves where all those 'should' thoughts are coming from can be so helpful. Would we say those things to a friend going through a tough time? Taking a moment to quieten the 'should' and welcoming ourselves in the reality of how it feels in the moment can feel very nourishing in its own way. There's a healing power to this acknowledgement without judgement. The answers of what to do next can come from this stage more abundantly than from the approach of harsh self-criticism. This feeling space can open up room for self-action, a possibility of what the future may hold in terms of new opportunities, leaving space in our hearts for something new. And grounding ourselves in what the future may hold with hope, releasing the grip of past reminders (yes, that includes the temptation to check their social media or reread old messages) and taking self-responsibility in creating beauty in our present moment because, in the end, this is all we have, and then repeating, repeating, repeating.

Without doubt, fear of the unknown can be overwhelming. It's human nature to seek what we know but being who you need in the moment to help you get through is a beautiful compassionate way to help. Time and the self-choices you make through this time to help the water flow past the rocks creates space for you to connect back to you, to flourish, to learn, to grow.

A ten-step plan to help you let go

Step 1: Acknowledge that there is a need to let go because holding on is causing too much discomfort and is no longer serving you. This step is powerful.

Step 2: With self-compassion, move towards letting yourself accept the reality that you can't change the past and that letting go is a way forward for you to flourish and improve your mental wellbeing.

Step 3: Acknowledge the attachment to the issue and your part in the need to let it go. Acknowledge the parts that you may find hard here. Sit with them. What are they trying to tell you?

Step 4: Allow yourself to feel any emotions that come up without judgement. Give yourself permission to grieve. Notice the sensations, however small, that your body may feel that could help bring ease.

Step 5: Shift your focus to your own personal growth. What are the things that bring joy? How can you move towards focusing on you?

Step 6: Prioritise self-care. This is a crucial step. What are the things that help you feel good about being you? The things that help you get out of your mind and into your body? These could be walks in nature, mindfulness, meditation, journalling, gratitude, coffee with a friend or movement.

Step 7: Allow space to reflect on everything being temporary, including feelings of loss of hope and sadness. These hard times will pass.

Step 8: Use some releasing techniques, such as writing the person a letter telling them how you feel, pour your heart out and write like no one will ever read it, then screw it up into a ball and throw it away. Or write yourself a letter as your parent self, offering advice and guidance on what you need to do. Keep this letter safe and read when you feel yourself struggling to let go.

Step 9: Self-reflect. What have you learned through this process? What parts that this process has revealed do you want to leave behind and what lessons do you want to take with you?

Step 10: Look towards the future. Allow yourself to dream. What are the possibilities, the new ventures, the new beginnings that could bloom now that space has been created?

How to challenge your thoughts

One of the hardest challenges of letting go is stopping what can sometimes feel like the never-ending cycle of rumination. The going back over things, taunting ourselves with what we should have done, how we could have done things differently, the hurt, the injustice. It can feel like a trap, and we can't find our way out. And the crux of the issue, too, is that we are only punishing ourselves, we are only stopping ourselves from flourishing. Our rumination isn't affecting the other person. And, sometimes taking that moment to realise that we are allowing someone else to have the power over how we feel, how we are living life, can be the wake-up call that we need to come back to self-responsibility and to taking the power back for our own lives.

Some steps that may help you reframe that rumination and help you take your power back:

Step 1: Acknowledge the cycle of thoughts and pay attention to the sensations that they are creating in your body, how they are affecting your emotions and your day-to-day wellbeing.

Step 2: Challenge the thoughts. It can be helpful here to remind yourself that thoughts are not facts. This can help you become in control of your thoughts as opposed to them feeling like they are in control of you. It can also be helpful here to ask yourself if this process of thinking is helpful. Acknowledge that staying stuck in rumination does not help you move forward.

Step 3: Reframe and replace the thoughts. How can you think about this situation differently? What will help you move forward? Even asking yourself the question of 'How do I want to feel?' can help create some movement forward in your thinking.

Step 4: Get out of your mind and into your body. Not as an avoidance to the issue but because rumination has a habit of going round and round in circles and unless we break the loop, it will keep going, sometimes relentlessly. So, move towards self-care. Deep soul-nourishing breaths, mindfulness, meditation, yoga, body scans or walks in nature all help to start to create a sense of safety in the body, calming our relentless thoughts. Remember that self-care practices are your best friend in so many situations.

Step 5: Reach out. If you are unable to stop the negative, self-limiting thought spirals, reach out for support to a friend you trust. Connection is deeply healing in helping us let go.

Step 6: Hold an awareness that those ruminating thoughts have a sneaky habit of coming back from time to time, so when they do repeat these steps, take a moment to reflect on how each one makes you feel and the sensations that come up.

Step 7: Come back to making your body feel safe, so that you can bring your nervous system out of fight/flight/freeze/fawn (protective states) and back to a safer place that feels like connection to self (as highlighted in Chapter Five). Tools such as tapping, body scans and breathwork can help here, as can guided meditations.

A meditation for letting go

Find a comfortable position, either lying down or seated, whichever feels right for you. If it feels safe, close your eyes and allow yourself to settle into stillness. Stay here for a while noticing the sensations in your body.

Now, gently rub your hands together until you feel some warmth. Place your hands on your heart and take a deep soul-nourishing breath in, followed by a long, slow exhale. Repeat. Notice your shoulders rise and drop with each breath. Notice your chest rise and drop. With each breath, notice yourself start to relax. Stay with this breath sequence. Let the breaths flow effortlessly.

Now, shift your focus to what you want to let go of – the hurt, the tension, or anything else. Bring it to your awareness. As you breathe in, imagine inhaling love, connection and safety. And as you exhale, release tension, doubt and emotional attachments. Breathe in safety, breathe out doubt.

Now, visualise your struggle to let go as a pebble. Imagine dropping that pebble into a calm lake. As the pebble touches the water, watch the ripples move outwards and slowly disappear, signifying your process of letting go. Each ripple represents the release of tension, moving further and further away until the water comes back to stillness, back to calm. Breathe into this stillness.

Notice how your body feels now, how your mind has calmed. Stay here for a while. Inhale gently and exhale. Inhale. Exhale.

And, when you're ready, gently bring yourself back to the present moment, becoming aware of your surroundings. Slowly bring your hands to your face, cupping your chin and reminding yourself that you matter. Take a moment to just be in this comforting space. Breathe in. Release. Breathe in. Release.

Journal prompts for letting go

- What is something that I am struggling to let go of?

- What impact is this having on me? How is it making me feel?

- Why am I finding it so hard to let go?

- What were the reasons behind the rupture/issue?

- What have I learned from this experience about myself?

- How would my life improve if I was able to let go?

- What sensations do I feel in my body when I consider being able to let go?

- What steps can I take to move towards releasing the attachment to the issue?

- What can I do in this moment to look after me?

- What brings me joy? How can I incorporate more of this into my life right now?

- Are there any boundaries I could set that would make this easier for me? (For example, stop keeping tabs on someone on social media.)

- What ways can I give myself self-compassion through this?

- Who can I reach out to for support?

When we come to the realisation that the only one hurting from the not letting go is ourselves, we can finally create space for healing, for release, for inner peace, for self-love.

Chapter Ten

On Hard Days

Gentle reminders for hard days:

- Focus on the next step in front of you, just that.

- Don't trust everything your mind is telling you.

- Listen to your body. What does it need?

- This too shall pass.

- It's OK to have hard days. It doesn't mean you're broken.

- You will get through this.

- Focus on what you can control and gently let the rest go.

- Can you offer yourself some compassion?

- Can you find a way to be who you need in this moment?

- Please don't struggle alone. Reach out.

- Remind yourself that you may not know how but you will find a way through.

How to stay hopeful when things feel hard

> **Neuroplasticity** refers to the brain's capacity to adapt and grow. It involves the formation of new neural connections, allowing the brain to reshape itself continuously, which can transform how our brains can react to various experiences, such as stress and trauma, facilitating better emotional regulation. For example, by regularly engaging in mindfulness exercises, individuals can witness structural changes, which lead to negative challenges being more manageable as they find new ways of approaching their life. Neuroplasticity enables us to see that personal growth and healing is possible.
>
> *definition*

Take a moment to acknowledge that hard days are inevitable. We all experience them. Every time we switch on the news or open a social media app, we are reminded of one crisis after another. A global pandemic, wars, political turmoil, societal ruptures, natural disasters. Adding to this, personal hardships, financial worries, poor health, relationship issues, grief, loss, trauma and ruptures. We can begin to see that hard days are thriving around us at a rather worrying speed.

Hard days are hard. I'm not here to say just think positively and you'll be fine. This isn't about toxic positivity. I've never known that to help anyone process anything, but I do vividly remember as a teenager reminding myself that it won't always feel like this on those days when the bullies were particularly unkind, and life felt like a lot. And that little mantra got me through. It was right, it didn't always feel like that. Those days did pass. Life happened. I didn't let those hard days win. There was so much beauty ahead of me. If only my 15-year-old self could see me now. Affirmations and mantras can have a hugely positive impact on how we cope. The words we speak affect how our body responds. Notice how your body feels when you say, 'That's it, I can't do this, I'm rubbish.' Chances are it folds in on itself, shoulders slump and a general lethargic heaviness may wash over you. Compare this to saying, 'It's OK, this is just a blip, I will get through this.' What does your body do? It may sit up a little taller, you may notice your breathing become a little deeper and you feel a little more empowered. The mind/ body connection here becomes very apparent. You may notice your nervous system coming out of fight/flight/freeze/fawn and moving back to connection with self.

We can truly be our own worst enemy, can't we? We rarely take a moment to even imagine that we could ever possibly feel better. But, we do. Think back to all those hard days you've experienced before. Those ones that have just felt too much, so much that you've wanted them over before they've even started. You've got through them. And this is not by any means dismissing how bad those hard days felt. But you found the personal resources to get yourself through. You did that, then, and reminding yourself of this in the moment can help you through another hard day. Those hard days have us forgetting that there's so much more beauty still to witness, so many wholesome conversations to be had, heart-warming moments to experience, so much awe to feel. So much more, more, more. Yet those days are there, waiting patiently in the wings for us.

And when we let go of the unhelpful internal dialogue that we are only meant to experience happiness and joy and accept that feeling frustration, disappointment, anger, upset and hurt are actually part of the spectrum of being human, we can hopefully begin to find a way to be who we need in that moment to help us get through, be it kind words, reaching out or any other tools that you have found that may help you. As opposed to when we use denial about feeling a certain way on those hard days and give ourselves a hard time for not feeling better or coping better, which, in turn, can leave us feeling less and not good enough. Think about how you feel when you switch your inner dialogue from harsh critical judgement to a dialogue that's more compassionate, caring and understanding.

Notice how you feel when you take a moment for yourself and acknowledge how you feel without judgement. Notice how you feel when you do more of the things that bring ease in the moment. Notice the sensations in your body here too.

Hard days are part of our normal human experience and the listening and the gentle curiosity are the tools that help us find a way through.

The compassionate approach of acknowledging that the day is hard, sitting with this acknowledgement, and then finding ways to feel more at ease in our body (think micro shifts and keep adding to them) instead of trying to force yourself out of it can help the body move through the day more comfortably.

Experiencing hard days and the tools we use to get through them helps us build our resilience and our resources for getting through the next hard day. We add to our lived experience of what helped and what didn't help. Avoidance doesn't help things go away, it just adds to suppressing emotions and the effect that can have on us as discussed in Chapter One. In fact, using these harder days to reflect and listen inwards to our body wisdom and to what it may be telling us can actually be a radical act of self-care as it will help guide us to the action we may need to take, such as reaching out, taking a step back, giving ourselves a break and looking after ourselves as best as we can.

Yet, hard days can take their toll on our mental health, leaving us feeling out of control. And whilst we can't limit hard days, we can build on our resilience to help us through. The more resilient you are, then the better able you are to cope with stress and anxiety, and to find a way to work through those harder times. It doesn't mean we won't experience hard days, but that we will have the tools and the emotional capacity to handle what life throws at us. And whilst we very much can't choose what life throws at us, we can choose how we respond, how we fight back, how we will choose our own path forward. Resilience is something within our own personal power that we can cultivate. Through a process of self-awareness, self-reflection, self-understanding and non-negotiable self-care, our resilience can flourish as we learn ways to best cope. For example, when faced with a stressful situation, we may learn that to take a pause and observe our emotions non-judgementally helps us respond with a calmer approach to the situation instead of reacting impulsively and lashing out. Building on this experience of what works and applying it to future stressors is a sign of cultivating resilience.

Turning to healthy choices on hard days can be challenging for so many reasons. On those hard days, we may be struggling with our emotions. This can influence our decision-making process where we may be more inclined to seek immediate comfort through unhealthy coping mechanisms, such as mindless scrolling, substance misuse and other self-sabotaging behaviours, without taking the time to consciously connect with whether it's a healthy choice for us or not. Our first reaction, when we are in discomfort, is survival and is rarely, 'Hang on, is this good for me?' Instead, we tend to unconsciously react and our body is more likely to ask, 'What did I do last time I felt this way to feel better, let's do that again,' unless we become more self-aware around our behaviours and challenge them. Once we build up a history of healthy behaviours that work, our body has a pool of healthy choices. Breaking unhealthy cycles can be challenging, especially on hard days when we feel drained and unable to think clearly. To begin fostering self-awareness of any self-sabotaging behaviours to cope on hard days is crucial (as we looked at in Chapter Seven). Taking small steps to bring patterns of behaviour to consciousness will help us move towards making healthier choices as we start to learn that, ultimately, it's those healthier choices that make us feel better longer term as we have less guilt, self-blame and negative self-talk. A short walk, a soul-nourishing breath, a small moment of gratitude, all have the power to release endorphins and start to improve your mood. Instead of aiming for grand changes, start with achievable self-care.

Ideas for your own hard days self-care toolkit

1. Give yourself a hug and offer yourself kind words.

2. Watch your favourite movie that brings joy.

3. Take some beautiful, soul-nourishing deep breaths.

4. Listen to some calming music or create a soothing playlist.

5. Read a book or listen to an audiobook.

6. Look out of your window and mindfully take in the scene that's happening outside.

7. Rest/nap/switch off.

8. Turn notifications off on your phone.

9. Create a cosy space at home, light candles, wrap yourself in a blanket, make your favourite drink.

10. Reach out to those who you feel safe with.

These are just examples but when we build our own self-care toolkit (you can use more ideas from Chapter Five here), it can be helpful to come back to these on those hard days and notice the sensations in our body as we move with love and care for ourselves. What are you adding to yours?

The importance of self-care when things feel out of control and as a resilience-building tool

I remember once having a particularly stressful week during the pandemic lockdown. As I clicked 'join meeting' for my weekly therapy meeting on Zoom (yes, therapists have therapy too), the words automatically spilled out: I recounted my week, where the torrent of things happening felt relentless, culminating in hearing myself say, 'I feel stressed and literally just want someone to give me a break from it.' 'It', I presume, was all the worry from living through a pandemic on top of everything else. Well, something like that. It was truly one of those weeks. And my therapist, who knows me incredibly well, let me use all my words up until I came to a natural pause (it took a while) and asked me two questions: 'How's your self-care been this week?' and 'What do you need right now?'

Those two seemingly simple questions brought me back into connection with myself and out of my fight/flight/freeze/fawn response. Hearing them was a light-bulb moment that has stayed with me since. How had my self-care been? Well, it had been non-existent. I'd made no time for striking a peaceful warrior pose on my yoga mat, I'd not been for my one walk per day and listened to a podcast, I'd not crept into the bathroom to light some candles, run a bath and locked the door for a delicious indulgent moment of time for me, and I'd most certainly not listened to a calming guided meditation. And it hit me. I'd not looked after myself. 'I' hadn't made an appearance on my to-do list once that week. And in answer to the second question of 'What do I need right now?', it was, without doubt, all of the above. Self-care shouldn't be for just when we need it. It should be part of our daily routine so that we avoid reaching such stressed-out levels, or at least, we should be popping self-care into our routine as a non-negotiable to help reduce the impact of stress. I am not saying just practise self-care and all your hard days will be non-existent. I know that's not how it works but a commitment to self-care does help us have access to more personal resources to better cope. Our glass is less full of the energy drainers. We have more capacity to cope.

On reflection, I've become more self-aware and am conscious that when I feel overwhelmed, there is a direct correlation with how much time I have or haven't made for myself. Do you feel that too? Those weeks when I've managed to roll the yoga mat out on more than one occasion tend to be handled a little better. I completely understand though, life is busy, and I know how hard it can be to put the things in place that are good for us but when we hold an understanding that we matter and that we cope better when we do care for ourselves, it kind of makes sense to take that self-responsibility and take better care of ourselves.

When I'm conscious that my first reaction to self-care is 'I haven't got time', I always reply with the gentle reminder, 'Then that's your reason for making it your priority this week.' A little self-talk goes a long way in those moments. And when you are really struggling with motivation, it can also be helpful to move your thoughts forward to how you usually feel after taking a walk or doing a yoga session. It can give you a temporary dopamine boost, which your body can crave to get more of and give you the little push that you may need to go do the thing. I appreciate that self-care looks different for everyone. We are all unique and where some things may relax some, they may not have the desired effect on others, so it's important that on those hard days, especially, that you do the things that help you but, where possible, come back to the basic question of 'What do I need right now to help?'

SELF-CARE PRACTICES TO HELP WITH HEALTHY NERVOUS SYSTEM REGULATION

- **Rest:** This can be anything that helps you feel content, it doesn't mean sitting doing nothing or sleeping, though naps and healthy sleep help, too.

- **Mindful breathing:** Bringing your attention to the inhalation and to the exhalation, noticing the rise and fall of your chest. Maybe take a moment to try this now. What do you notice?

- **Experiencing nature:** This can be walks or taking a moment to stand at your window and take in the sounds of the outside. The sounds of the birds, the feel of the breeze, the temperature of the air, taking in the movement of the clouds in the sky or watching the stars. Breathe into this. Immerse yourself for a few moments. Even listening to soundscapes of nature on your phone have been proven to bring relaxation.

- **Making your body feel safe:** Through body scans, somatic exercises and breathwork.

- **Gratitude:** Deep embodiment of the practice works to help bring healthy nervous system regulation.

- **Nourishing meals:** Cook something you enjoy. Take time to prepare and devour.

- **Keeping hydrated:** This simple act does wonders for our mental wellbeing as it is essential in optimising brain health.

- **Self-compassion:** Think carefully about the way you treat yourself on those hard days. Treat yourself as you would a friend. Gentleness over judgement. Be who you need.

- **Finding small moments of joy:** Maybe it's reading, maybe it's watching your favourite movie. Whatever it is, give yourself permission to do it on repeat and notice the tiny shifts that may happen within and repeat.

- **Movement:** Whatever your choice is. From simple stretching to a walk to a run to rolling out your yoga mat.

- **Reaching out:** Connection helps our mental wellbeing more than we are consciously aware of.

Whilst it can feel almost impossible to do the things that are good for us on those hard days, sometimes the act of choosing one from this list can help create a tiny shift within. A tiny shift that says movement forward is possible. It will help you to be able to care for yourself through the difficult times. We have an increased ability to connect with what the emotions attached to the bad days are trying to tell us when we have the capacity to listen.

Steps towards building resilience and creating personal resources

Step 1: Acknowledge that hard days are inevitable and that they will pass. Holding on to this can be tricky but can be so beautifully healing too. Notice the sensations in acknowledging this, however small. Maybe a small movement from the protective states of fight/flight/freeze/fawn into a connection back to self. Even the smallest of shifts can help you see that movement out of fight/flight/freeze/fawn is possible.

Step 2: Learn to gently reframe thoughts with added compassion. For example, 'That date was terrible. I'm never going to meet anyone. I'm going to be single forever', reframed as, 'That person wasn't for me, but I know that I'm going to find someone else because I have wonderful qualities that I know the right person will like.' Or, 'I'm really worried about having that difficult conversation.' Reframed as, 'I know that this conversation will help things longer term and my opinion matters, too.'

Step 3: Incorporate non-negotiable self-care practices, such as yoga, meditation, baths, walks in nature, gratitude, connection with friends, time for you. This step matters more than we consciously realise, helping our nervous system to be able to healthily regulate. The effect of this step on providing capacity, creating space for ourselves and, therefore, resilience is huge.

Step 4: Look after your physical health basics, such as exercising, eating healthily, prioritising rest and sleep. These things may seem basic, but they matter hugely in building our overall resilience and caring for ourselves in a deeply nourishing way.

Step 5: Let go of unrealistic expectations. Set small, achievable and realistic goals in all areas of your life, both short and long term. You're more likely to accomplish these small goals, which will help you to be able to celebrate small wins more frequently. This can help have a positive impact on your resilience. On a bad day, it could be, 'I'm just going to do the bare minimum today and release the pressure on me.' Notice how your body reacts to these words over, 'I just need to get on with it and achieve what I normally do on a good day.' Or even smaller, 'I will get up and make my bed.'

Step 6: Become more self-aware. What are your strengths and weaknesses? What are the things that make you feel like you can't cope? What are the tools that you do have access to that help you cope better? What have you learned about your past self in difficult times before? Use this step to reflect a little deeper on how you got through hard times before. Add those tools to your mental coping toolkit for next time. You know you best, so you know what works best.

Step 7: Acknowledge that resilience is a process and takes time, but continued cultivation helps it to keep blooming.

Gratitude as a radical act of self-care

I've come to believe that gratitude is like magic. It's my go-to tool every single time when things feel a lot. It's a tool I can have instant access to if I just remember to use it. That and breathwork. But the magic of gratitude is that the very act of bringing our awareness to the things we are grateful for, however small, triggers the release of neurotransmitters, such as dopamine and serotonin, which are associated with more positive emotions, such as happiness, joy and contentment. Those feel-good hormones literally flood through our body enabling us to feel more balanced and calmer. Our nervous system can start to feel safer. And let's be honest, on those hard days, our nervous system can feel anything other than safe. It can feel incredibly activated (switched on), which impacts how we cope overall as in fight/flight/freeze/fawn. We may feel more stressed, anxious or low in mood. When we feel safer and are able to healthily regulate (hold emotions and self-soothe), we can cope a little better and, in some cases, a lot better as we move towards making healthier choices. Gratitude has the power to build resilience deep within.

Let's try something here. Take a moment to consider someone that you're grateful for in your life. Picture them. Imagine they are with you. Think about the way they make you feel. The sound of their voice. The times you've been together. Stay here for a while in this moment. What do you notice in your body? What sensations? Any release of tension? Or tingling? How about your breathing? What about your jaw? For me, I noticed I smiled, and then I smiled again noticing I smiled. I took a deeper inhalation of breath, my jaw relaxed and my entire body felt flooded with contentment. I could feel something in my heart/chest area that felt fuller, but in a good way full not tense full. How about you? Did you feel something too?

Gratitude can be miraculous. When we deeply connect to the practice and embody it, instead of brushing it off as another 'woo woo' self-care practice, we can truly reap its benefits. Gratitude is about restoring our peace of mind where negativity threatens to destroy it. Deep embodiment of gratitude can bring with it those feelings associated with peace of mind that simple positive thinking doesn't even come close to. Gratitude doesn't have to be big things. It can be tiny things that create the smallest of shifts. A connection back to something that feels safer. Keep building on those. Keep looking towards the light. Keep adding to your feel-good source of gratefulness. And I know that in some instances it can be incredibly difficult to feel gratitude, so this is not a reminder to 'look on the positive side.' Rather, it is an offering of gentle encouragement that gratitude can serve as a deep act of self-care when you may just need it. Your nervous system will be encouraged to healthily regulate, which is what is much needed on those hard days.

Three good things

This simple tool helps cultivate resilience longer term:

1. At the end of each day, take a little time to reflect on the positive moments that happened. Allow the feelings you experienced to flood over you. Sit for a while and let those feel-good feelings come back into your body. Notice the sensations, the way your breath changes, how your limbs feel, how your muscles may relax, even just a little bit. Bottle these feelings as a memory resource to come back to.

2. Choose three good things that happened, no matter how small. Such as a smile from a stranger, a text from a friend, the appearance of sunshine after many days of rain.

3. Write these three good things down in a journal dedicated to this purpose, including how they made your body feel and use this journal as a regular resource to tap into when you need to connect back to those feelings.

Journal prompts for hard days

- What am I feeling right now? If I could name the emotion, what would it be?

- What sensations do I feel in my body? What are they trying to tell me?

- Reflect on why today feels difficult. What's the main reason for the feelings?

- What do I need to help me through this?

- How can I offer myself compassion?

- When I think of being kinder to myself, how does my body respond?

- What three things am I grateful for? How does that gratitude make my body feel?

- How have I coped with hard days before?

- Who can I reach out to?

- What are three acts of self-care that I can do today to nurture myself through this?

Of course, hard days challenge us, but just like those tiny little flowers that grow through those cracks in what looks like the most uninhabitable concrete, so can you. Look for the light. Don't stop looking for that light.

On Comparison

Chapter Eleven

We shouldn't get caught up in comparison because:

- we never truly know what someone is going through behind the scenes.

- it can take us away from living our own life.

- it can lead us to doubting ourselves.

- it can affect our self-worth.

- it can take affect our self-confidence.

- it can take us away from choosing ourselves.

- it can create feelings of negativity within.

- it doesn't help us live a life that feels good on the inside.

- it doesn't enable us to flourish.

- it can take the joy out of living our very own lives.

Understanding comparison

'Comparisonitis' is not an official word but a term coined in recent years. It is the tendency to excessively compare oneself to others, which can lead to self-judgement, feelings of not being good enough, low self-esteem and overall discontentment with one's own life. Comparisonitis causes people to require constant validation as they measure themselves against others in terms of social status, achievements and appearance, and generally has a negative impact on someone's mental wellbeing.

definition

I was as young as seven years old when I first became familiar with the concept of comparison and why we shouldn't get caught up in it. My aunt was visiting from Devon, and I was squashed up next to her in the back of the car on our way out to dinner. It was summer and we were driving through a beautiful village. Out of the window, I caught sight of the most stunning sprawling home with immaculate lawns sweeping down to meet the village road. The house was spectacular but that wasn't what initially caught my eye, it was the rather wonderful red climbing frame in the garden. It even had a double swing. I was seven years old. It was beautiful and whilst I was very lucky to have a garden at home, I didn't have a climbing frame. And I remember so clearly saying, 'Oh, the girl who lives there is SO lucky!' And without missing a beat, my aunt replied and gently said, 'Oh, but dear Helen, you know nothing about that girl, you've never even met her. She may have had a terrible accident last week and not be able to use that climbing frame.' And she was so right. I remember this story clearly as forming one of my core beliefs in how I see the world and I'm grateful for her lesson. We never truly know what someone's life looks like or, more importantly, how it feels from what they show us.

We literally make up stories to fill in the blanks from what someone shows us. We've all been there, scrolling through social media, seeing someone's ideal life and thinking that they must have it all (whatever 'all' is). Rarely do we stop to consider that maybe they struggle with something in their life, maybe they have anxiety or depression (because anxiety and depression does not have a type or a look) and that the smile they share on social media is covering immense struggles, maybe worry, as well as fear of how people are going to react to their photo. Yet we rarely make up stories that maybe they haven't got it altogether, even though it's highly likely that that story would be somewhat closer to the truth. Being human is messy and it's rarely perfect, whatever social media or appearances may have you believe. In a world where social media dominates our lives, comparison has escalated on a much larger scale, so much so that it's hard not to find yourself occasionally drawn into comparing yourself. Comparison is human nature. And it has two components: upwards and downwards. This is how we move towards valuing our worth in the social circles we are in. Upward comparison means we find ourselves feeling less than someone, which is where the issues of lack of self-confidence and self-worth come in. It may manifest in phrases like 'I haven't got their size house, so I must be less successful than them, and they must be happier and more sorted.' Downwards comparison, on the other hand, is looking at our self-worth based on someone who we deem to be inferior. Goodness, it's not a beautiful side of human nature, though, is it?

Upward comparison shows how comparison can be used for growth, if used in a healthy way. For example, you might see an immaculate tidy house on social media and reflect on how yours isn't that perfect. It could be the motivation you need to tidy a small part of the mess you're sitting in. (I once sorted out my cutlery drawer after seeing someone show their immaculately placed silverware on Instagram! Seriously!) Or maybe it could inspire a deeply honest conversation with yourself. Do you even want a tidy house? Or are you quite happy sitting in your cosy, book-sprawling environment, with the children's toys everywhere, which shows how enrichingly full your life is?

Sometimes, what we see and what we *think* we want isn't always what we necessarily really want. The process of self-reflection can help show you the answer. Come back to the truth that is inside of you. You don't have to be like someone you see on social media just because you think that's how you should be. You may be happy with your life in ways that you hadn't previously considered that you were. Take a moment to notice where your inner narrative of 'I should be' comes from. Is it from the pressure of social media and societal narratives around perfection, or is it a deeper inner truth?

On the other hand, you might see someone start a new course that inspired them. You might notice they're lifted and have a new zest for life, encouraging you to find a course that would inspire you. If they can do it, why not you? Comparison, used as inspiration, can be hugely beneficial. It's when we use it with judgement of the other person or against ourselves in a negative way, thinking we aren't good enough, that comparison can become more of a problem in our life that we may want to get a little more curious about. What are the feelings of comparison masking? What's beneath? But it's this level of self-awareness that can help move us from feeling stuck, resentful and judgemental to ways that support us in feeling more aligned, compassionate and understanding to both ourselves and, of course, others. We never know their true story, but we do know ours and that's where we can do more self-work and exploration to learn more about ourselves.

I witness the negative aspects of comparison in the therapy room with feelings such as not being good enough, guilt, remorse and reduced self-esteem, self-worth and confidence. As well as immense frustration and dissatisfaction with people's own lives dominating and preventing people moving forward to see the value of their own journey and a future where their life feels good to them. But it's wonderful to also witness clients growing through self-work and being able to catch themselves thinking, 'Oh, that's just me comparing again, isn't it? Hang on whilst I just come back to connecting with myself and what I do know to be true.' And, even, 'What ways can I be inspired? What is this comparison really telling me? And what unmet need is this touching on?' I delve more into these unmet needs in the following section.

The impact of comparison and how to flourish instead

The reasons for comparison will differ for everyone, but comparison is often underpinned by low self-worth, poor sense of self or unhappiness. It can be the starting point for some self-work to ensue. Naming the feeling that comparison may bring up and identifying the unmet need can be enlightening work. Maybe there's a need for seeing more of the world, doing more, being happier or having more financial security. Maybe there's a need for more closeness in a relationship, or a deep inner loneliness is highlighted when scrolling and comparing reveals examples of people out and having fun with friends whilst you're home without an invite. When you repeatedly put yourself in front of upward comparison, the impact on your nervous system to feel dysregulated takes you deeply away from feelings of contentment, connection and alignment with self.

Doing the self-work and gently exploring the reasons behind the comparison as a starting point can help you feel better in the long term. Seeing yourself and the comparison through the lens of gentle curiosity, so that you can start to make small changes, through self-work or setting boundaries – such as less time scrolling and more time working on a new project to bring inspiration – will help towards longer term improved mental wellbeing. Contentment, connection and alignment with self are needed in abundance if we want to flourish. Without it, feelings of low self-esteem, manifesting in saying to yourself, 'I'm not good enough', 'My life isn't where I want it to be' or 'I'll never get there' will impact your nervous system. You may initiate an immediate stress response, such as increased anxiety or lethargy, irritation or frustration. Allowing ourselves to be consumed by the cycle of comparison can leave us stuck in a stress response leading to longer term symptoms of anxiety and depression, such as sleeplessness and decreased motivation. Our nervous system becomes more dysregulated, which continues to affect our overall mental wellbeing and the self-choices we make, or lack of them. When we view life from a protective state of fight/flight/freeze/fawn, which comparing can instigate, we impinge on our connection back to self, and so exacerbate all the symptoms that come with a dysregulated nervous system.

Imagine scrolling through social media and comparing yourself. You may start to consider feelings of not being good enough, thin enough, happy enough, rich enough. What sensations do you notice? Do you feel yourself coming away from connection to yourself and more into those protective states of fight/flight/freeze/fawn? For me, I notice my throat constrict, a slight tightening of my jaw, a tension in my shoulders and a different feeling in my chest. Now come back to connection with yourself. A deep breath, some words of affirmation such as, 'I will not compare myself to strangers on the internet', or some gentle encouragement, 'Actually, I feel inspired.' What sensations do you notice now? Can you feel your body soften and come back into safety? This is a gentle exercise which shows you how comparison can stimulate the fight/flight/freeze/fawn in an everyday way.

COMPARISON CYCLE EXAMPLE

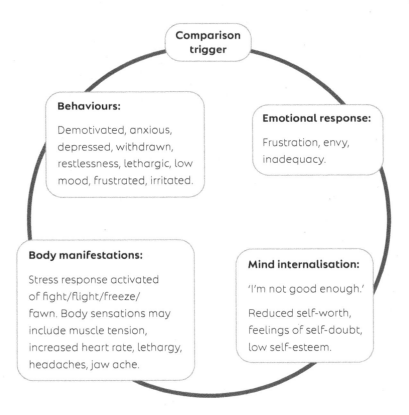

Comparison can keep us stuck in a loop, unless we do something to break the cycle. I always feel that the visualisation of this cycle can help us see where we can make the changes to stop the treadmill feeling of comparison and looping thoughts, as well as behaviours that do not promote our mental wellbeing.

For example, if we do nothing, then nothing changes, and we stay caught in the cycle. Stopping one of the steps in the cycle – either by removing the triggers, reaching out for help, focusing on self or reframing the negative thought spiral with inspiration over comparison – can be a key step in activating our nervous system to move into a more connected state and away from a stress response.

It's from this regulated state that we can make better informed, caring self-choices, such as gently exploring why we have felt activated by the comparison, and relying on the tools we have to self-regulate. The shifts in mood state may be tiny but just noticing the movement of the nervous system regulating from fight/flight/freeze/fawn back to connection to self and a place of safety can be the momentum we need to move away from the cycle and towards a state of flourishing.

How to break free from the trap of comparison

Step 1: Do you often get caught up in comparing yourself?

Yes

No

Go to step 2.

Step 2: Does this comparison bring you inspiration and motivation?

Yes

No

Maybe take some time to reflect on how this is helping you grow. What changes have you made?

Continue to step 3.

Step 3 is overleaf

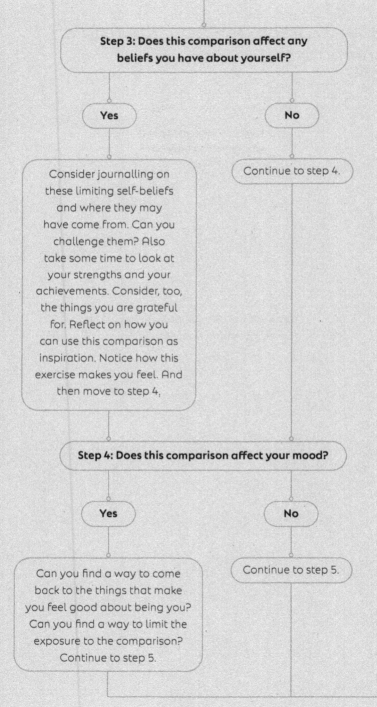

Step 3: Does this comparison affect any beliefs you have about yourself?

Yes

No

Consider journalling on these limiting self-beliefs and where they may have come from. Can you challenge them? Also take some time to look at your strengths and your achievements. Consider, too, the things you are grateful for. Reflect on how you can use this comparison as inspiration. Notice how this exercise makes you feel. And then move to step 4.

Continue to step 4.

Step 4: Does this comparison affect your mood?

Yes

No

Can you find a way to come back to the things that make you feel good about being you? Can you find a way to limit the exposure to the comparison? Continue to step 5.

Continue to step 5.

Step 5: Is this comparison based on knowledge of the other person's whole life?

Yes

Take some time to reflect here on your own journey and acknowledge that we never fully know the in-depth stories of others, however close we are to them. Think about how others in your life don't know your full story. Continue to step 6.

No

Reflect that appearances are deceiving, and people rarely share their struggles whatever their appearance may show. Continue to step 6.

Step 6: Are there ways that you can use these feelings of comparison as inspiration?

Yes

Use this inspiration to make healthy choices that benefit your mental health and wellbeing going forward, focusing on your own strengths, too.

No

Consider taking some time to reflect on how the negative feelings of comparison are not benefitting your mental wellbeing and looking at ways to use self-responsibility to limit comparison traps. Consider using gratitude and practising self-care to boost self-worth and self-esteem, which will help limit the negative effects of comparison. Reach out for help if you continue to struggle. There may be a deeper reason that needs some unpacking.

How to come back to connection to self

External validation is the need to seek approval or recognition from others to be able to feel that we are enough, that we are worthy and that we are accomplishing things in life. It typically manifests from low self-worth, poor sense of self and unhappiness in one's own life.

Internal validation happens when we learn to accept ourselves for who we are and enable ourselves to see our own strengths, hold our own values and a healthy judgement of self, and are able to connect with our own truth of who we are.

definition

Comparison is a normal part of human behaviour, but that doesn't mean it sits comfortably with us or that we want to let it in too much. It can highlight our need to be validated and symbolises a deep human desire to belong and feel connected to others. This can sometimes leave us reeling towards those feelings that we aren't enough, that we don't have enough friends, that we don't fit in and can leave us feeling disconnected from our own life and from ourselves. Comparison takes us away from the life we are living. And as hard as comparison can seem to be to escape from, due to the volume of glimpses into other people's lives that social media has opened up, there are tools we can use to lessen its impact when we feel its grip tightening. These tools help bring us back into alignment with ourselves.

TOOLS TO BEAT COMPARISON

Self-awareness: Let's be honest, comparison never makes us feel great, does it? So, take a moment to come back to some self-awareness. Reflect on your thought patterns here and the emotions you feel and your behaviours when you find yourself comparing. Notice how the process maybe doesn't make you feel lifted or inspired. Take a moment to identify what started the thoughts of comparison and notice the direct influence it has on your mental wellbeing. Bringing this to awareness can be the first step to listening to what the comparison is trying to communicate with you, and also to taking a degree of self-responsibility in moving on from the comparison and challenging any negative thought patterns that may arise.

Focus on your own life: Once you have acknowledged the effect that the comparison is having and the initial triggers, bring yourself back to your own path and the journey your life has taken. Reflect on your achievements, the difficulties you've overcome, your own lived experiences. Notice how your body responds when you come back to yourself in this way. What sensations do you notice? Bring in gratitude here, too, remembering the powerful healing qualities of this action. Use the energy that may arise from this process to move forward. Maybe you want to set some goals for yourself or some boundaries around limiting exposure to the triggers, be it social media or particular groups of people that may evoke those feelings. Come back to the things that make you feel good about being you, about living the life you live and repeat, repeat, repeat. This coming back to connection with yourself can help open up the opportunities for how you can live the life you want to live. Maybe seeing healthy relationships may encourage you to take some small steps to work on your own relationship. Bring the focus back inwards. Always looking outwards at others takes you repeatedly further and further away from yourself.

Love yourself for who you actually are: This deep act of self-love enables you to start the process of embracing your imperfections as being deeply human and real. And whilst you reflect on the nature of less than perfect humans as a normality, remind yourself that everyone feels these insecurities about themselves, whatever they may portray to the world. We are more similar than we may believe. But imagine a world where people could be transparent about their deemed imperfections, how refreshing to hear someone say how they truly feel, as if opening up the flood gates for others to be able to say, 'Me too.' How refreshing for their transparency to be met with compassion and care. It's up to us to be the change. It's up to us to be the brave ones that step away from the societal norms of pretending that we have it all together. I know it takes bravery. I know it's incredibly complex to deconstruct in a few words on a page but a little curiosity about this can go a long way. Let's start the conversation and keep it flowing. Let's help the next generation not be so caught up in being tough, enable them to embrace imperfections, enable them to feel good enough, to be the kind receptor to someone expressing how they really feel about themselves.

Curate your social media: With social media being undeniably a source of 'comparisonitis', give yourself permission to make it something beautiful to curate. Follow accounts that inspire, lift and motivate you. Mute or unfollow those accounts that make you feel anything other than the best version of yourself. Get deeply honest with yourself about how you feel when you scroll. Can you step away for a while if you notice comparison creeping in and come back to self-awareness again? This is a vital step worth popping on repeat in the trap of breaking 'comparisonitis': awareness around what the comparison is bringing up for you and the fact that it's taking you away from yourself. Keep coming back to you. Keep coming home.

Embody self-compassion: Take a moment to reflect on what self-compassion means to you. Notice the sensations that come up; yes, even the uncomfortable toe-curling ones. Where are those messages coming from? Come back to being on your own side here. Watching our self-talk and offering self-parenting words of comfort, kindness and gentleness can help create the shift within to move away from the uglier feelings that comparison can leave us with. Use the self-compassion to go deeper inwards. Using a little gentle curiosity around the feelings the comparison brought up and sitting with them without self-judgement may help bring some answers to the icky feelings. We talked about what comparison may be uncovering earlier in this chapter. What is it uncovering for you?

Come back to inspiration: Be inspired. Finding ways to be inspired by people can be a beautiful gift of motivation. Having a mindset of 'I could try that, too' can be incredibly soothing to the nervous system compared to the nervous system being activated by the triggered feelings of comparison, such as 'I'm not good enough' or unhealthy jealousy. Using the comparison as a guide to the qualities and characteristics in others that you aspire to develop yourself can be an example of healthy modelling.

> **Healthy modelling** is the behaviour that inspires and encourages others to adopt positive practices in their own lives, helping to create a nurturing and supportive community. *definition*

We can be the ones to change the negative societal narrative around comparison. Let's embody comparison as a driving force of self-compassionate movement forward, of checking back in with ourselves that we are where we want to be, as well as an appreciation of our own humanity.

EXERCISE

Affirmations to help let go of comparison

I am on my own beautiful unique journey.

The world needs me to be me.

I need me to be me.

I will not compare myself to strangers on the internet.

Comparison only reduces me and doesn't further me.

I will reframe comparison as inspiration.

I will use my journey to inspire myself and others.

In each moment, I have the personal power to be who I want to be.

I get to choose.

Someone else's path is not my path. My path is my path.

I will cultivate a life that feels good on the inside.

My life is worth my own beautiful attention, nurturing and nourishment.

Journal prompts for letting go of comparison

- What are the areas in your life that you frequently find yourself comparing? How does it make you feel?

- How does the impact of comparison affect your self-confidence and self-esteem? What behaviours do you find yourself engaging in after comparing?

- Is there another way you can reframe comparison? Is there a message here guiding you to take action?

- Can you find a way to use comparison as inspiration?

- Take a moment to write a list of your own strengths.

- What three words would your loved ones use to describe you?

- What would your life look like if you didn't compare? How would it feel?

- How can you find a way to support and celebrate others? How would that make you feel?

- How does it make you feel when others support and celebrate you?

- What is one step you can take today to move away from comparing yourself and move towards embracing your life fully?

Those moments that move you away from your own beautiful path stop you from creating a life that feels good to you on the inside and inside is where the magic lies. Come back home to what makes you feel good, makes you breathe with more ease, makes you fall in love with your own life a little more. Looking outwards will never create the same inner peace that looking inwards does. Keep nurturing, keep growing, keep blooming.

On Choosing You

Chapter Twelve

Choose you so that you can:

- breathe more freely.

- live a life that feels good on the inside.

- be on your own side.

- flourish.

- deeply understand yourself.

- feel connected to yourself.

- let go of guilt.

- experience a different level of inner peace.

- feel free.

- be a better version of yourself for others.

- embody being who you were always meant to be.

What does choosing you mean?

Choosing yourself is about being wondrously on your own unique side and meeting yourself with gentle compassion, always. Take a moment to let this sink in as you embrace the notion of being there for yourself. Of being for yourself and not against yourself. Of tuning in to your inner self, by truly listening and understanding the whispers of self-awareness with gentle encouragement, kindness and support. Of knowing your needs and cultivating the tools to meet them. Of choosing you to be the best version of yourself. Of meeting yourself where you're at and reminding yourself that you may not know how but you'll give it your best attempt to get through something together for yourself. Of being your very own trusted support system as a gentle nurturing guide to being the best version of yourself.

Self-limiting beliefs are those little whispers in our minds that hold us back from being the happiest version of ourselves. They can stem from past experiences, upbringing, societal pressures and other people's opinions of us. Holding an understanding of where they come from and gently challenging them as opposed to believing them is key in self-work, so that we can move to fully choosing ourselves, too. A simple question can be, 'Is this even true?'

definition

Choosing yourself can be challenging, so let's just consider those we care about in our lives. Reflect on times you've witnessed someone you love being rejected, being excluded, feeling lost. Maybe you've seen them settle with being someone's 'maybe' and that's enough for them, waiting and hoping anxiously and patiently to be their first choice. Maybe you've seen them trying so hard in a relationship, but their trying isn't reciprocated or even genuinely appreciated. Maybe you've seen them not follow their dreams due to the disapproval of others, allowing external opinions to dictate their path, their journey. Maybe you've seen them lash out, project their hurt or withdraw as a result. Maybe you've witnessed their pain. How often have you wished that they would have put themselves first, been on their own side, valued themselves more highly and ultimately chosen themselves? It can be disheartening to witness their lack of self-value, their unresolved attachment wounds, their inability to prioritise their own needs, their lack of choosing themselves, which may result in repetitive patterns that leave them undervalued or lacking self-worth.

Perhaps you even see some of this in yourself? It's truly heartbreaking, isn't it? Because, as humans, we all have an innate longing to belong, to connect, to fit in and to feel wanted. It's a fundamental aspect of our blueprint for survival. But seeking connections with the wrong people, who don't bring that sense of safety, peace, alignment and ease, will never provide the genuine sense of belonging and mental wellbeing that can be achieved through the right connections.

Take a moment to reflect on the different emotions you feel when you are in the presence of those who truly see you and appreciate you, versus those who make you feel less than. By cultivating this gentle awareness, you've reached the pivotal starting point for embarking on a journey of making life choices that prioritise your own wellbeing. You're beginning to recognise the significance of such choices in bringing inner harmony rather than dysregulation. From a nervous system perspective, choosing yourself matters. Countless opportunities for happiness, contentment and living a life that resonates and feels like home are missed, if we don't think that we matter and if we don't fundamentally choose ourselves.

Reflect upon a time when you may not have been able to show up for yourself and prioritise you. Consider a situation when your

partner may have upset you and you found it hard to communicate. Instead of sitting with them and working through an
issue, your stress response of fight/flight/freeze/fawn might've
kicked in, causing an ineffective self-soothing choice. Maybe
your choice of behaviour – such as passive aggression, negative
self-talk, self-sabotaging, excessive alcohol or substance misuse,
binge-eating, endless scrolling, withdrawing, impulsive shop-
ping – led you to feel more disheartened than soothed. Or maybe
you ignored the hurt in a desperate attempt to just go back to
how it was before the hurt. Ignoring your needs. Putting your
partner first. But in fact, showing them that you don't think that
you matter. This is an example of you not choosing you.

Now imagine that in that moment, you chose yourself, you
acknowledged that you'd been hurt, understood your stress
response, noticed the pattern of behaviour was unhealthy and
were able to come to a place of self-understanding. Imagine
choosing a different coping mechanism and meeting yourself with
love and compassion, identifying your needs; maybe your choice
of coping mechanism would be healthier and the self-sabotaging narrative wouldn't kick in so easily. And maybe by meeting
your needs and not suppressing the emotional response that your
body stores and struggles to cope with long term (as explored
in Chapter One), you could understand the messages that your
body is trying to communicate and look to a way of listening to
the actions they may be telling you to take. Can you see how
the resulting scenarios would play out for both here? Which one
feels closer to being on your own side? Which one feels kinder?
Which one feels like a leaning into the truth of you? But can
you also see how choosing you takes deep self-understanding and
self-work? And can you see the benefits of this long term on so
many levels? Themes of this have been woven throughout the
chapters of this book, helping you to, ultimately, choose you.

I understand how challenging this can be in the moment, so a simple, yet not so simple, tip is to catch yourself and ask if this is the choice you want to make right now? Is there a different choice you'd prefer? Is this the time you'd like to change the way you respond? It might not help immediately but this continued inner dialogue, with practice, can become your new guide, your new way of choosing healthily for yourself, too.

To actively choose ourselves, we must embark on an inward journey of self-reflection to seek an understanding of the factors that shape who we are. This involves cultivating self-awareness, challenging self-limiting beliefs and assuming the role of nurturing parent to yourself – a connection that perhaps you may have neglected or not even been aware of in the past. It entails gently tapping into your inner wisdom, to the guiding voice within. I do appreciate that this requires both courage and a genuine desire to want to choose yourself, as well as an exploration of any resistance that may be there to this process. But if not choosing yourself means less satisfaction, less happiness, less authentic connection to others and compromised mental wellbeing, then choosing yourself at least offers a new path towards contentment.

Take a moment to reflect here on those times when you've felt genuinely most like yourself. What have those connections to others in your life felt like in that moment? How has your energy been received? How has this feeling like the best version of you influenced those around you? How has your capacity to cope been affected? How have you been able to be more supportive of others in that moment too? Maybe you've been there for them more in a more present and compassionate way. And how have you felt about yourself in those moments? Lighter? Freer? A healthier, happier version of you? You do matter, too. Just as you want those you care about to choose themselves so that they feel that they also matter.

Why it can be difficult to choose you

Choosing yourself isn't always an easy process. It sounds attractive in theory, doesn't it? Going through life, picking out the things that feel good to us on the inside, meeting our needs at every step? But the reality is very different. For some of us, we may not have been modelled this as a way of caring for ourselves growing up. We may even fear that we may be rejected by those closest to us if we choose ourselves. And with our inherent survival need of wanting to fit in, to be accepted and to belong, this can make choosing ourselves even more complex as we end up becoming sensitive and moulding ourselves into what is deemed acceptable, so that we can fit in as best we can. Or maybe we have developed people-pleasing behaviours because of our earlier lived experiences, where we learned that our needs were less important than others, which makes choosing ourselves feel very unfamiliar and perhaps even unsafe. Remember, our nervous system craves familiarity even when that isn't the best thing for our mental health and wellbeing. It can take some work to undo these unhelpful thought processes that have become hardwired into our lives and nervous system (including self-awareness, self-reflection, challenging inner belief systems or seeking more professional help).

Society's messages imply that putting ourselves first is considered selfish, so it's no wonder we have feelings of guilt and shame when we do. These emotions can become barriers, preventing us from choosing ourselves. Consequently, we may find ourselves making choices that don't feel right, simply because we believed someone else's needs were more important. As a result, we end up neglecting our own wellbeing. How many times have you said yes when you would much rather have said no, because you felt guilty? Yet, if we wouldn't want those whom we care about to experience this, why would we allow it for ourselves?

I hope you're beginning to see why choosing yourself can be such a challenge. It involves a process of gradually releasing the resistance that may have held you back in the past from making this choice. Take a moment to reflect on how the idea of meeting your own needs makes you feel. You might experience a sense of tranquillity. Notice the sensations in your body. Even if you're unsure about how to choose you and to meet those needs right now, simply being open to the idea of doing so in the near future can be a healing experience in itself. Or maybe the thought of choosing yourself leaves you feeling uncomfortable. This may be an invitation to explore the reasons behind the discomfort. If we continue in our familiar patterns of behaviour (of lack of self-care and not making choices that align with our core values of who we are) and maintain this by not changing, we are actively choosing to remain not on our own side, and nothing will truly transform. We will continue to make unhealthy choices to our detriment and the detriment of others. We are relational beings, so our choices impact others more than we consciously realise.

Us not choosing ourselves may result in us feeling depleted, which means we are unable to show up fully for others who need us.

I'm reflecting here on those who make life-changing choices – maybe in their 40s or 50s or 60s, or even in their 30s – who are criticised for having a mid-life crisis or reliving their youth. Or those who start the journey of healing later in life and they are viewed sceptically by some (more often than not by those who have had a hold on them for years). But maybe they are finally seeing the changes in their life they want to make. Maybe they are regretting the choices they've made where they have never even considered that meeting their own needs was a possibility. Maybe they are finally freeing themselves of past attachment wounds, people-pleasing behaviours, societal pressures, self-limiting beliefs and choosing themselves. Let's celebrate these choices rather than judge.

You may have come across those poignant social media posts featuring wise words from the elderly. Often, their messages urge us to live a life with fewer regrets, emphasising the importance of choosing happiness and, ultimately, choosing ourselves more wholeheartedly. I know the details of these words are over simplified, and as with everything, each scenario takes some deeper unpacking and understanding, but the message is clear, isn't it? We get one chance at this thing called life. Let's strive to make it one that resonates deeply. And if that means honouring our needs, being on our own side a little more and cultivating more inner ease with ourselves and with our interactions with those around us, then it's imperative that we encourage everyone to choose themselves a little more. This isn't about selfishness, despite the misconceptions often associated with self-care and self-love. It's about recognising our intrinsic worth and acknowledging that our needs are just as significant as those of others. Everyone holds value. Everyone matters.

And when we come to accept that choosing ourselves is not selfish, it allows us to prioritise our own wellbeing and happiness. Neglecting to choose ourselves can lead to feelings of dissatisfaction, resentment and burnout as we continuously put others' needs before our own. This is self-neglect, leaving us feeling unfulfilled and disconnected from our authentic selves. Choosing ourselves is an essential step towards building a healthier, happier and fulfilled life, the beautiful ripple effect of which is explored later in this chapter.

How to actively choose you

Self-reflective prompts to consider when working through the steps below to choose you:

- How does your body respond? What feels like it fits and what needs a little more gentle curiosity?

- How does the prompt resonate for you? Does it feel encouraging, or do you notice resistance?

- What needs come up as you work through the steps below? More self-love? A need to reach out?

- How can you use these ideas to take one tiny step, towards making a shift to choosing you?

> **A gentle note for you:** How often do we just sit and ponder who we are and what our needs may be? This is just a small act of choosing ourselves. It doesn't have to be a grandiose display. And with each tiny step, something shifts, something new is created. It can be beautiful. And as Nietzsche said, 'Become who you are.'

STEP 1. PRACTISE SELF-REFLECTION

Use this step to reflect on where you're at in your life, the choices you've made. Reflect on the areas of your life that you're happy with, the relationships, your work, your purpose, your sense of self. Are you feeling authentic, fulfilled and aligned? Is your current situation aligning with your core values? And then move to reflect on the areas that you'd like to change in some way to benefit your mental wellbeing. Maybe you're struggling with anxiety, and you'd like to feel a little more at ease in your day.

Can you include a step that enables you to look at this more? Can you reach out or find a small way to start the healing process? Or is there an issue in your relationship that keeps repeating itself and which you'd like to move forward from? Gently explore this with curiosity over judgement. And as something arises, see if you can offer yourself some guidance in that moment. One tiny step.

STEP 2. DEVELOP SELF-AWARENESS

Connect a little more with the self-reflection by moving to an awareness of how the issues in your life are making you feel: the emotions they bring up or the behaviours that may ensue because of the issues. Ways to enhance self-awareness can be through meditation, journalling, mindfulness and creating space for you and your thoughts. Are there any patterns that you can identify? Any contributing factors that cause the issues you'd like to change? Go gently.

STEP 3. EXPLORE AVAILABLE RESOURCES

Read books, articles, blogs. Listen to podcasts. Watch documentaries. Follow registered therapists online. This may help towards shifting any stuck perspectives, help bring enlightenment and enable you to understand yourself, as well as be a guide for enabling you to make healthier self-choices. Remember, baby steps. Try adding something new. Try it on for size as such and see what fits. Discard what doesn't.

STEP 4. PRACTISE NON-NEGOTIABLE SELF-CARE

Make this a priority. Consider the things that are good for you. The science-backed things that improve mental wellbeing, like meditation, journalling, yoga, breathwork, nature, movement, etc. It can be good to be mindful here of any shifts within as you start to bring these practices into your weekly life. Also, see if you can take a moment to notice how you feel when you let these practices subside a little. Practising self-care like you matter can be a deeply connecting activity. Remember that you need you as do those who love you, so a little self-care is necessary not selfish.

STEP 5. CHOOSE SELF-RESPONSIBILITY

Take a moment to be the person you need. Consider writing a letter to yourself outlining the care you need to take to look after you and the importance of choosing yourself. This can be a deeply motivating and compassionate self-practice that helps you value yourself a little more, as well as coming back to the essence of choosing yourself and being on your own side. A letter of pure self-love. Use this step as an action prompt. What are the small things that you could do to move towards choosing yourself more today?

STEP 6. GET A LITTLE CURIOUS AND NAME ANY RESISTANCE

It can be helpful in this step to name the reasons why you find choosing yourself hard. Maybe it's guilt? Maybe choosing yourself wasn't modelled to you as a child? Or perhaps you have often fallen into people-pleasing behaviours? Or change feels scary? Or you're not quite sure how to prioritise yourself? Explore with gentleness a little more deeply. Holding an awareness that choosing you longer term will lead to overall mental wellbeing through the very process of learning to identify and meet your needs. The process can also help limit regrets longer term. There are no wrong answers. This is just the story of you. Get curious. Get creative.

STEP 7. AND, LASTLY, REVIEW AND REFLECT

Come back to the act of self-reflection. What's working? What's not? Where do you need more support? What other actions do you need to take to feel like you're choosing you in a healthy way? What are the blocks to choosing you? Is there any resistance? What can you celebrate? What shifts can you notice within, however small? What can you keep building on? What step needs more work? More support? This stage can help bring empowerment and self-confidence as you take charge of your choices.

The beautiful ripple effect of choosing you

Picture someone with their friend who is going through a difficult time and needs some support. However, this person finds it challenging to be fully present because they stayed up late working on a deadline, resulting in minimal sleep. They had then intended to wake up early and rejuvenate themselves with a walk in nature before meeting their struggling friend. Unfortunately, their plans were interrupted when their parents called, wanting to catch up. Consequently, they spent an hour on the phone, feeling too tired to fully engage in meaningful conversation. By the time they finally meet their friend, they have hardly taken a moment for themselves, and are feeling tired, irritable and unable to be who they would want to be for their friend and what their friend needs.

Now consider an alternative scenario where the person chooses themselves, and boundaries and self-care were prioritised. Imagine work boundaries being put in place, ensuring they got sufficient sleep and were well rested. They might have then chatted with their parents about the need for a rejuvenating walk and scheduled a time for a longer catch-up. As a result, they would have met their friend in a calmer, relaxed and refreshed state, enabling them to offer more empathy and compassion benefitting the friend immensely compared to the first scenario. The ripple effect is a source of strength.

Let's imagine another scenario whereby someone had not followed their dreams but had instead followed the dreams of their parents. They could then have taken a course at university that did not align with their own passions and dreams. As a result, the pressure of the workload becomes too much, and they find themselves surrounded by peers who do not share similar interests because it wasn't their first choice. This could then lead to chronic stress kicking in causing them to not get the level of degree they were hoping for. Consequently, their career options become limited, and they find themselves in a job where they feel unhappy and unfulfilled. This may be a contributing factor in the development of symptoms of anxiety and depression. The overall life satisfaction of the person would be reduced, impacting their day-to-day life and their relationships. This could lead to a draining impact on friends and family as the person's unfulfilled demeanour may mean they can't show up as their contented and aligned self. Imagine this versus someone who was encouraged to follow their dream, supported and celebrated, enabling them to take a career in something they felt passionate about. Their overall life satisfaction improved, as well as their general mental wellbeing, so that they felt happier in the relationships around them and could show up as themselves and not as a draining energy that could bring everyone around them down.

These contrasting scenarios show how choosing yourself can have a profound effect on both you and those around you. Consider how you feel around those people who lift and inspire and have an energy that is fulfilled versus those who are negative about everything around them, projecting on to others and not supporting themselves or able to support you in any way. It's clear to see how the underlying current of not having chosen themselves could have a ripple effect outwards as opposed to examples where they have taken and been encouraged to take self-responsibility to make choices that met their own needs.

Choosing yourself does not mean neglecting the needs of others but serves as a reminder that you do indeed matter, too.

Meeting your own needs, understanding yourself and showing up for yourself enables you to help meet others' needs, understand them and have more empathy and compassion, as well as show up for others in a kinder and more present way.

Having this mindset that moves away from thinking that choosing ourselves is selfish can be helpful in the self-responsibility of actively making choices in our lives that not only meet our needs but that feel aligned, authentic and nourishing. Whilst people may have our best interests at heart, it's important to consider that only you know what you truly need, what feels right, what connects and what makes you feel most you. The journey to choosing you may be complex, challenging, uncomfortable and difficult to navigate at first but with compassion, practice and gentle curiosity, as well as noticing and listening inwards to how your body reacts, just maybe you will find that it gets a little easier.

Some gentle examples of what choosing you may look like to help you get started: choosing to spend more time doing a hobby you love, prioritising self-care such as reading before bed or taking a bath, saying no to more work commitments, spending an evening in on your own instead of feeling the pressure to go out, choosing to rest when needed, listening to your body a little more, setting personal boundaries maybe around phone use or limiting late nights, spending more time with people who energise you. These gentle choices can add up to making big differences to how your days go. Notice how one small step may impact on the others. Notice who reacts to your choices. Cultivating an environment of healthy choosing and respect of others' healthy choices can truly have the most beautiful ripple effect. Setting that wonderful example of taking time for us teaches our next generation that it's not selfish to have needs and to meet them. Maybe then, going forward, we will see a generation that is supportive, less resentful, less judgemental and more compassionate, caring and present. It starts with us, it always does.

Affirmations for when you're struggling to choose you

I can be a kind person and still choose me.

I am allowed to say no without feeling guilt.

My needs matter, too.

I give myself permission to choose a life that makes sense to me.

I choose people who choose me.

I choose people who celebrate and support my growth.

I will honour my self-responsibility in looking after myself.

I choose to be my most authentic self.

I encourage others and welcome others choosing themselves.

I respect other people's boundaries and choices.

My happiness is my responsibility.

I will seek my own validation.

I trust that to feel like I belong requires me to be my most authentic self.

Showing up for myself teaches others how to show up for me.

Showing up for myself encourages others to show up for themselves.

I trust that I know what choices I need to make.

I am the author of my story and I deserve to be the main character.

I am the only person who knows what my needs are and how they can best be met.

I will meet myself with compassion and release judgement.

I am deserving of living a life that feels good to me.

I will let go of fear, shame and guilt and embrace choosing me.

Journal prompts to help choose you

- What are some needs in your life that aren't currently being met?

- How is this not meeting them making you feel?

- Describe how you imagine it would feel and what your life would look like if they were met.

- What are the things that are currently holding you back from living the life you'd like to be living?

- How could you make room to move these obstacles that are holding you back?

- How does your current life make you feel on the inside?

- What are some steps you could take to improve this feeling?

- Write down and describe three things that you love about yourself? Notice how writing those made you feel.

- What value do you bring to the relationships in your life?

- Reflect on how you matter in the relationships in your life.

- What is one small step you could take today to choose yourself a little more?

Choose you for your own mental wellbeing. Choose you because you matter, too. Choose you so that you can live a life that feels good and makes sense to you. Choose you so that you can be the best version of yourself to others. Let that beautiful act of choosing you ripple out in abundance into the world around you, not just for your generation but for all those beautiful generations to follow.

Final Thoughts

By understanding yourself, you create space for you to begin to understand others; to see their humanness; to hold their vulnerability; to meet them with compassion.

And for me, this is the essence of why I wanted to write this book. To bring awareness to what makes us fundamentally us. How we are shaped by our experiences. How we learn, evolve and, I hope, bloom from our interactions with others. That we are not broken. We are not too much. We are not alone. And through self-exploration, self-awareness, self-understanding with gentle compassionate curiosity, we can make choices of how we take how we have been shaped, forward. We are the owner of that choice. That is our story. We get to write the next part. And in bringing this into the space of this book, I hope you gained some clarity in knowing that we are deeply complex beings, with a need for being accepted and to feel like we belong. All of us. And I hope that in bringing to light these parts of being human, you got to see a glimpse of the humanness in others. Choosing ourselves can help give us that beautiful insight. I hope you felt it.

And whilst this was a book for you and a book to encourage you to choose you, it was written as a guide for you to understand that in understanding yourself at a deeper level, by the sheer act of choosing yourself, you can find a way to understand others and to choose them, too. To ultimately thrive, we need beautiful, authentic, safe connections and those are easier to find when we have learned to choose ourselves in all that that entails. We aren't meant to do life alone. We are wired for connection. And I see the ripple effect of choosing ourselves in my clients each day. Their relationship with themselves improves, their relationship with others improves, their friendships become closer, their sense of value flourishes and they live lives that feel more aligned and fulfilled, and they live them from a place of ease. It takes time. It's a process. But the shifts are beautiful to witness. Choose you.

Resources

SOME FAVOURITE BOOKS

Why Love Matters by Sue Gerhardt
The Body Keeps the Score by Bessel van der Kolk
Waking the Tiger: Healing Trauma by Dr Peter Levine
Attached by Dr Amir Levine and Rachel Heller
Anchored: How to Befriend Your Nervous System Using Polyvagal Theory by Deb Dana
Polyvagal Card Deck by Deb Dana
Why Has Nobody Told Me This Before? by Dr Julie Smith
A Manual for Being Human by Dr Sophie Mort
The Drama of Being a Child by Alice Miller
The Mind Manuel by Dr Alex George
The Myth of Normal by Gabor Maté with Daniel Maté
Unshame: Healing Trauma-Based Shame through Psychotherapy by Carolyn Spring
No Bad Parts: Healing Trauma and Restoring Wholeness with the Internal Family Systems Model by Richard Schwartz

SOME FAVOURITE WEBSITES

Psychologytoday.com
Nicabm.com
Verywellmind.com
Psychcentral.com
Positivepsychology.com
Mind.org.uk

SOME FAVOURITE PODCASTS

The Class
Sounds True
Expanded by To Be Magnetic
Feel Better, Live More
Transforming Trauma
Dear Therapists
Huberman Lab
On Purpose
The SelfHealers Soundboard

SOME FAVOURITE MEDITATIONS

The Insight Timer App
Jack Kornfield
Dr Joe Dispenza
Tara Brach
Sarah Blondin
Davidji
Dr Kristin Neff

SOME MISCELLANEOUS ADDITIONS

The world's longest scientific study of happiness
    (The Grant Study) from the Study of Adult Development
    at Harvard Medical School
Neuroplasticity video by Sentis: https://www.youtube.com/
    watch?v=ELpfYCZa87g

SITES TO HELP FIND A PRIVATE THERAPIST

British Association for Counselling and Psychotherapy (BACP)
BetterHelp
Counselling Directory
Psychotherapy.org.uk

LOW-COST THERAPY OPTIONS

UK Counselling Network
Headstrong Counselling

MENTAL HEALTH CHARITIES

Mind
CALM (Campaign Against Living Miserably) for men
   aged 15–35
Young Minds
Anxiety UK
Samaritans
Nightline Association (for students)
Beat (for eating disorders)
Rethink Mental Illness
Mental Health Foundation

Acknowledgements

This feels very humbling to write and I'm finding it hard to know where to start, so I'm starting at what I feel was the beginning of the evolving process of *Choose You*.

Without my beautiful Instagram community showing up for me daily and so generously engaging and sharing my posts, then I'm not sure this book would ever have been written. Your daily presence and deep commitment to doing the work has been such a huge inspiration behind the creation of me writing this book for you. Thank you, thank you, thank you.

Such heartfelt thanks to Sam Jackson, my editor. You will never know just how much my heart soared when you contacted me back in late October 2022 – 'Would I like to explore writing a book?' you asked. There was only one answer! Sam, thank you for being the vision behind *Choose You*. It has been an absolute dream to work with you. Who knew writing a book would be such a pleasure? Your gentle reassurance, guidance and trust in me helped this come to life more than you could know. Thank you.

But I didn't get just one editor, I was immensely lucky to have the wonderful Evangeline Stanford working with me every single step of the way. Evangeline, I am beyond grateful for your continued belief in *Choose You* and your unrelenting help. This book is what it is because of you, and I am honoured that you were part of the *Choose You* team. Thank you.

Thank you also to the people behind the scenes at Penguin: Jasleen and Shikha, and to Purvi, Vicki and Jonathan – what a team, thank you! Oh, and special thanks to the designer of the cover, Claire Rochford – my heart actually skipped a beat when I saw it – pure beauty!

Thank you, also to my agent, Jane Graham Maw. Jane, your ever calming supportive presence through all the intricacies of what it means to actually write a book is deeply appreciated. Being able to hand over the "complicated stuff" most definitely helped keep my nervous system regulated throughout the process and that was no mean feat! Your support and belief in *Choose You* means the world.

And to my clients. My wonderful, courageous clients. Your bravery, your growth, your commitment to therapy is truly awe-inspiring and I am so grateful for the journey you allow me to be on with you. This book is also because of you. Keep choosing you.

And, finally, to my dearest friends and family who have been there behind the scenes, checking in on me, cheering for me. You know who you are, thank you. *Choose You* was so much easier to write with you by my side. Immense gratitude.

About the Author

Helen Marie is a London-based therapist with her own private practice working with clients internationally. Helen is passionate about helping people develop the skills they need to understand themselves at a deeper level, and is the creator of accessible and relatable advice about self-work, trauma, attachment and relationships on Instagram and TikTok at @h.e.l.e.n.m.a.r.i.e. *Choose You* is her first book.